D1053210

Be
Your
Best
Self

Be Your Best Self

Thomas S. Monson

Deseret Book Company
Salt Lake City, Utah, 1979

© 1979 Thomas S. Monson
All rights reserved
Printed in the United States of America
ISBN 0-87747-787-6
Library of Congress Catalog Card
Number 79-54782

*Dedicated to my
father and mother,
the late
G. Spencer and
Gladys Condie Monson*

Contents

Foreword

For some time I have had on my desk a small sign that simply says "DO IT."

As I look at this slogan, I often think of Elder Thomas S. Monson, one of my colleagues among the General Authorities, for to me he is truly a "do it" man.

I have come to know Elder Monson intimately since he was called to the Council of the Twelve in 1963, and I regard him as one of the Lord's most able servants. He has exemplified through his years of service a steady devotion to the Lord's work that is worthy of emulation.

It seems appropriate that this volume of his messages and teachings should be titled *Be Your Best Self*, for I believe that is the message of Elder Monson's ministry. He travels the world in behalf of the Church, and wherever he goes he is able to bring out the best in people. He is an effective leader because he has this ability to develop and cultivate the best in others.

As an Apostle of the Lord Jesus Christ, Elder Monson is filled with the pure love of Christ, and he radiates this to others. People love him because he loves them. His witness to the world is one of love and understanding.

As a community and business leader, Elder Monson has helped many others to achieve. His career before becoming a General Authority was one of personal achievement as well as motivating others to excel. His guiding hand is still felt in numerous community and business endeavors, and thus he continues to make a valuable contribution to the lives of people, members and nonmembers alike.

As a husband and father, he is also making great contributions, for his children are growing and maturing in responsible ways. He has inspired them to do their best at home, in the Church, and in their careers.

Elder Monson is a remarkable human being. The Lord has called him to great service in the Church, and he is truly giving of his best. I earnestly hope that this compilation of his wisdom and teachings will help you, the reader, to reach your maximum potential and to be your best self!

President Spencer W. Kimball

I

ASK IN
FAITH

1

*H*opeless Dawn—Joyful Morning

London, England, is steeped in history. Who has not heard of Trafalgar Square, Buckingham Palace, Big Ben, Westminster Abbey, or the River Thames? Of lesser renown, yet priceless in value, are the truly magnificent galleries of art situated in this city of culture.

One gray, wintry afternoon I visited the famed Tate Gallery. I marveled at the landscapes of Gainsborough, the portraits of Rembrandt, and the storm-laden clouds of Constable. Tucked away in a quiet corner of the third floor was a masterpiece that not only caught my attention, but also captured my heart. The artist, Frank Bramley, had painted a humble cottage facing a wind-swept sea. Kneeling at the side of an older woman was a grief-filled wife who mourned the loss of her seafaring husband. The spent candle at the window ledge told of her fruitless, night-long vigil. The huge gray clouds were all that remained of the tempest-torn night.

I sensed her loneliness. I felt her despair. The hauntingly vivid inscription that the artist gave to his work told the tragic story. It read: A HOPELESS DAWN.

How the young widow longed for the comfort, even the reality, of Robert Louis Stevenson's "Requiem":

Home is the sailor, home from the sea,
And the hunter, home from the hill.

For her and countless others who have loved and lost dear ones, each dawn is hopeless. Such is the experience of those who regard the grave as the end and immortality as but a dream.

The famed scientist Madame Marie Curie returned to her home the night of the funeral for her husband, Pierre Curie, who was killed in an accident in the streets of Paris, and made this entry in her diary: "They filled the grave and put sheaves of flowers on it. Everything is over. Pierre is sleeping his last sleep beneath the earth. It is the end of everything, everything, everything."

The atheist Bertrand Russell adds his testament: "No fire, no heroism, no integrity of thought and feeling can preserve an individual life beyond the grave." And Schopenhauer, the German philosopher and pessimist, was even more bitter. He wrote: "To desire immortality is to desire the eternal perpetuation of a great mistake."

In reality, every thoughtful person has asked himself this question: Does the life of man continue beyond the grave?

Death comes to all mankind. It comes to the aged as they walk on faltering feet. Its summons is heard by those who have scarcely reached midway in life's journey, and often it hushes the laughter of little children. Death is one tragic fact that no one can escape or deny.

The venerable, perfect, and upright man named Job, centuries ago, pictured death in these words: "As the waters fail from the sea, and the flood decayeth and drieth up: So man lieth down, and riseth not: till the heavens be no more, they shall not awake, nor be raised out of their sleep." (Job 14:11-12.)

But Job, like multitudes of his fellow men, rebelled at this conclusion. Turning away from the depressing spectacle of death's seeming victory, he uttered the triumphal cry: "Oh that my words were now written! oh that they were printed in a book! That they were graven with an iron pen and lead in the rock for ever! For I know that my redeemer liveth, and that he shall stand at the latter day upon the earth. . . . In my flesh shall I see God." (Job 19:23-26.)

And who can help but be inspired by the clarion call of the apostle Paul as he declared: "I am persuaded, that neither death, nor life, nor angels, nor principalities, nor powers, nor things present, nor things to come, Nor height, nor depth, nor any other creature, shall be able to separate us from the love of God, which is in Christ Jesus our Lord." (Romans 8:38-39.)

Perhaps no statement in scripture more dramatically reveals a divine truth than Paul's epistle to the Corinthians: "For as in Adam all die, even so in Christ shall all be made alive." (1 Corinthians 15:22.)

Frequently, death comes as an intruder. It is an enemy that suddenly appears in the midst of life's feast, putting out its lights and gaiety. Death lays its heavy hand upon those dear to us and at times leaves us baffled and wondering. In certain situations, as in great suffering and illness, death comes as an angel of mercy. But for the most part we think of it as the enemy of human happiness.

The plight of the widow, for instance, is a recurring theme throughout Holy Writ. Our hearts go out to the widow at Zarephath. Gone was her husband. Consumed was her scant supply of food. Starvation and death awaited. Then came God's prophet with the seemingly brazen command that the widow woman should feed him. Her response is particularly touching: "As the Lord thy God liveth, I have not a cake, but an handful of meal in a barrel, and a little oil in a cruse: and, behold, I am gathering two sticks, that I may go in and dress it for me and my son, that we may eat it, and die." (1 Kings 17:12.)

The reassuring words of Elijah penetrated her very being: "Fear not; go and do as thou hast said: but make me thereof a little cake first, and bring it unto me, and after make for thee and for thy son. For thus saith the Lord God of Israel, The barrel of meal shall not waste, neither shall the cruse of oil fail. . . . And she went and did according to the saying of Elijah. . . . And the barrel of meal wasted not, neither did the cruse of oil fail."

This same widow then lost her precious son to the enemy death. But the God of Heaven heard her plea and, through His prophet, restored to her the lad.

Like the widow at Zarephath was the widow of Nain. She too lost her son. She too had him returned to her and to life— whole. A gift from the Lord Jesus Christ.

But what of today? Is there comfort for the grieving heart? Does God remember still the widow in her travail?

Not far from the Salt Lake Tabernacle lived two sisters. Each had two handsome sons. Each had a loving husband. Each lived in comfort, prosperity, and good health. Then the grim reaper visited their homes. First, each lost a son; then the husband and father. Friends visited, words brought a measure of comfort, but grief continued unrelieved.

The years passed. Hearts remained broken. The two sisters sought and achieved seclusion. They shut themselves off from the world that surrounded them. Alone they remained with their remorse. Then there came to a latter-day prophet of God, who knew well these two sisters, the voice of the Lord, which directed him to their plight. Elder Harold B. Lee left his busy office and visited the penthouse home of the lonely widows. He listened to their pleadings. He felt the sorrow of their hearts. Then he called them to the service of God and to mankind. Each commenced a ministry in the holy temple. Each looked outward into the lives of others and upward into the face of God. Peace replaced turmoil. Confidence dispelled despair. God had once again remembered the widow and, through a prophet, brought divine comfort.

The darkness of death can ever be dispelled by the light of revealed truth. "I am the resurrection, and the life," spoke the Master; "he that believeth in me, though he were dead, yet shall he live: And whosoever liveth and believeth in me shall never die." (John 11:25-26.)

This reassurance, yes, even holy confirmation of life beyond the grave, could well be the peace promised by the Savior when He assured his disciples: "Peace I leave with you, my peace I give unto you: not as the world giveth, give I unto you. Let not your heart be troubled, neither let it be afraid." (John 14:27.)

"Ye believe in God, believe also in me. In my Father's house are many mansions: if it were not so, I would have told you. I go and prepare a place for you . . . that where I am, there ye may be also." (John 14:1-3.)

Out of the darkness and horror of Calvary came the voice of the Lamb, saying, "Father, into thy hands I commend my spirit." (Luke 23:46.) And the dark was no longer dark, for He was with His Father. He had come from God and to God He had returned. So also those who walk with God in this earthly pilgrimage know from blessed experience that He will not abandon His children who trust in Him. In the night of death His presence will be "better than a light and safer than a known way."

The reality of the resurrection was voiced by the martyr Stephen as he looked upward and cried: "I see the heavens opened, and the Son of man standing on the right hand of God." (Acts 7:56.)

Saul, on the road to Damascus, had a vision of the risen, exalted Christ. Later, as Paul, defender of truth and fearless missionary in the service of the Master, he bore witness of the risen Lord as he declared to the saints at Corinth: "Christ died for our sins according to the scriptures; . . . he was buried, and . . . he rose again the third day according to the scriptures: . . . he was seen of Cephas, then of the twelve: After that, he was seen of above five hundred brethren at once. . . . he was seen of James; then of all the apostles. And last of all he was seen of me." (1 Corinthians 15:3-8.)

In our dispensation this same testimony was spoken boldly by the Prophet Joseph Smith, as he and Sidney Rigdon testified: "And now, after the many testimonies which have been given of him, this is the testimony, last of all, which we give of him: That he lives! For we saw him, even on the right hand of God; and we heard the voice bearing record that he is the Only Begotten of the Father—That by him, and through him, and of him, the worlds are and were created, and the inhabitants thereof are begotten sons and daughters unto God." (D&C 76:22-24.)

This is the knowledge that sustains. This is the truth that comforts. This is the assurance that guides those bowed down with grief out of the shadows and into the light.

Such help is not restricted to the elderly, the well educated, or a select few. It is available to all.

Several years ago, the Salt Lake City newspapers published an obituary notice of a close friend—a mother and wife taken by death in the prime of her life. I visited the mortuary and joined a host of persons gathered to express condolence to the distraught husband and motherless children. Suddenly the smallest child, Kelly, recognized me and took my hand in hers. "Come with me," she said, and she led me to the casket in which rested the body of her beloved mother. "I'm not crying, Brother Monson, and neither must you. My mommy told me many times about death and life with Heavenly Father. I belong to my mommy and my daddy. We'll all be together again." The words of the Psalmist echoed to my soul: "Out of the mouth of babes . . . hast thou ordained strength." (Psalm 8:2.)

Through tear-moistened eyes, I recognized a beautiful

and faith-filled smile. For my young friend, whose tiny hand yet clasped mine, there would never be a hopeless dawn. Sustained by her unfailing testimony, knowing that life continues beyond the grave, she, her father, her brothers, her sisters, and indeed all who share this knowledge of divine truth, can declare to the world: "Weeping may endure for a night, but joy cometh in the morning." (Psalm 30:5.)

With all the strength of my soul, I testify that God lives, that His Beloved Son is the first fruits of the resurrection, that the gospel of Jesus Christ is that penetrating light that makes of every hopeless dawn a joyful morning.

2

The Way Home

Overlooking the azure blue waters of the famed Sea of Galilee is a historic landmark—the Mount of Beatitudes. Like a living sentinel with an eyewitness testimony, this silent friend seems to declare: "Here it was that the greatest person who ever lived delivered the greatest sermon ever given—the Sermon on the Mount."

Instinctively the visitor turns to the Gospel of Matthew and reads: "And seeing the multitudes, he went up into a mountain: and when he was set, his disciples came unto him: And he opened his mouth, and taught them." (Matthew 5:1-2.) Among the truths He taught was this solemn statement: "Enter ye in at the strait gate: for wide is the gate, and broad is the way, that leadeth to destruction, and many there be which go in thereat: Because strait is the gate, and narrow is the way, which leadeth unto life, and few there be that find it." (Matthew 7:13-14.)

Wise men throughout the generations of time have sought to live by this simple statement.

When Jesus of Nazareth personally walked the rock-strewn pathways of the Holy Land, He, as the good shepherd, showed all who would believe how they might follow that narrow way and enter that strait gate to life eternal. "Come, follow me," He invited. "I am the way."

Little wonder that men did tarry for the outpouring of the Holy Ghost on the day of Pentecost. It was the gospel of Jesus Christ that was to be preached, His work that was to be done, and His apostles at the head of His church who were entrusted with the work.

History records that most men indeed did not come unto Him, nor did they follow the way He taught. Crucified was the Lord; slain were the apostles; rejected was the truth. The bright daylight of enlightenment slipped away, and the lengthening shadows of a black night enshrouded the earth.

One word and one word alone describes the dismal state that prevailed: apostasy. Generations before, Isaiah had prophesied: "Darkness shall cover the earth, and gross darkness the people." (Isaiah 60:2.) Amos had foretold of a famine in the land—"not a famine of bread, nor a thirst for water, but of hearing the words of the Lord." (Amos 8:11.) Had not Peter warned of false teachers bringing damnable heresies, and Paul predicted that the time would come when sound doctrine would not be endured?

The dark ages of history seemed never to end. Was there to be no termination to this blasphemous night? Had a loving Father forgotten mankind? Would He send forth no heavenly messengers as in former days?

Honest men with yearning hearts, at the peril of their very lives, attempted to establish points of reference, that they might find the true way. The day of the reformation was dawning, but the path ahead was difficult. Persecutions would be severe, personal sacrifice overwhelming, and the cost beyond calculation. The reformers were like pioneers blazing wilderness trails in a desperate search for those lost points of reference which, they felt, when found would lead mankind back to the truth Jesus taught.

When John Wycliffe and others completed the first English translation of the entire Bible from the Latin Vulgate, the then church authorities did all they could to destroy it. Copies had to be written by hand and in secret. The Bible had been regarded as a closed book forbidden to be read by the common people. Many of the followers of Wycliffe were severely punished and some burned at the stake.

Martin Luther asserted the Bible's supremacy. His study of the scriptures led him to compare the doctrines and practices of the church with the teachings of the scriptures. Luther stood for the responsibility of the individual and the rights of the individual conscience, and this he did at the imminent risk of his life. Though threatened and persecuted, yet he declared boldly: "Here I stand. I can do not otherwise. God help me."

John Huss, speaking out fearlessly against the corruption within the church, was taken outside the city to be burned. He was chained by the neck to a stake, and straw and wood were piled around his body to the chin and sprinkled with resin. Finally he was asked if he would recant. As the flames arose, he sang, but the wind blew the fire into his face, and his voice was stilled.

Zwingli of Switzerland attempted through his writings and teachings to rethink all Christian doctrine in consistently biblical terms. His most famous statement thrills the heart: "What does it matter? They can kill the body but not the soul."

And who cannot today appreciate the words of John Knox: "A man with God is always in the majority"?

John Calvin, prematurely aged by sickness and by the incessant labors he had undertaken, summed up his personal philosophy with this statement: "All our wisdom comprises basically two things . . . the knowledge of God and the knowledge of ourselves."

Others could indeed be mentioned, but a comment concerning William Tyndale would perhaps suffice. Tyndale felt that the people had a right to know what was promised to them in the scriptures. To those who opposed his work of

11

translation, he declared: "If God spare my life, I will cause a boy that driveth the plough shall know more of the scripture than thou doest."

Such were the teachings and lives of the great reformers. Their deeds were heroic, their contributions many, their sacrifices great—*but they did not restore the gospel of Jesus Christ*.

Of the reformers one could ask, "Was their sacrifice in vain? Was their struggle futile?" I answer with a resounding "No!" The Holy Bible was now within the grasp of the people. Each man could better find his way. Oh, if only all could read and all could understand. But some could read, and others could hear; and every man had access to God through prayer.

The long-awaited day of restoration did indeed come. But let us review that significant event in the history of the world by recalling the testimony of the plowboy who became a prophet, the witness who was there—even Joseph Smith.

Describing his experience, Joseph said: "There was in the place where we lived an unusual excitement on the subject of religion. It . . . became general . . . [and] created no small stir and division amongst the people, some crying, 'Lo here!' and others, 'Lo there!' . . .

" . . . I was one day reading the Epistle of James, first chapter and fifth verse, which reads: *'If any of you lack wisdom, let him ask of God, that giveth to all men liberally, and upbraideth not; and it shall be given him.'*

"Never did any passage of scripture come with more power to the heart of man than this did at this time to mine. It seemed to enter with great force into every feeling of my heart. I reflected on it again and again, knowing that if any person needed wisdom from God, I did; for how to act I did not know, and unless I could get more wisdom than I then had, I would never know; for the teachers of religion . . . understood the same passages of scripture so differently as to destroy all confidence in settling the question by an appeal to the Bible.

"At length I came to the conclusion that I must either remain in darkness and confusion, or else I must do as James directs, that is, ask of God. . . .

"So, in accordance with this, my determination to ask of God, I retired to the woods to make the attempt. It was on the morning of a beautiful, clear day, early in the spring of eighteen hundred and twenty. . . .

"I kneeled down and began to offer up the desire of my heart to God. . . .

" . . . I saw a pillar of light exactly over my head, above the brightness of the sun, which descended gradually until it fell upon me.

" . . . When the light rested upon me I saw two Personages, whose brightness and glory defy all description, standing above me in the air. One of them spake unto me, calling me by name and said, pointing to the other—*This is My Beloved Son. Hear Him!*" (Joseph Smith—History 1:5-17.)

The Father and the Son, Jesus Christ, had appeared to Joseph Smith. The morning of the Dispensation of the Fulness of Times had come, dispelling the darkness of the long generations of spiritual night. As in the creation, light was to replace darkness; day was to follow night.

From then to now, truth has been and is available to us. Like the children of Israel in former times, endless days of wandering now can end with our entry to a personal promised land.

Today we may hear God's prophet speak—even President Spencer W. Kimball. Today there goes forth from him an invitation to people throughout the world: Come from your wandering way, weary traveler. Come to the gospel of Jesus Christ. Come to that heavenly haven called home. Here you will discover the truth. Here you will learn the reality of the Godhead, the comfort of the plan of salvation, the sanctity of the mar-

13

riage covenant, the power of personal prayer. Come home!

From our youth many of us may remember the story of a very young boy who was abducted from his parents and home and taken to a village situated far away. Under these conditions the small boy grew to young manhood without a knowledge of his actual parents or earthly home. Within his heart there came a yearning to return to that village called home. But where was home to be found? Where were his mother and father to be discovered? Oh, if only he could remember even their names, his task would be less hopeless.

Desperately he sought to recall even a glimpse of his childhood. Then, like a flash of inspiration, he remembered the sound of a bell that, from the tower atop the village church, pealed its welcome each Sabbath morning. From village to village the young man wandered, ever listening for that familiar bell to chime. Some bells were similar, others far different from the sound he remembered.

At length the weary young man stood one Sunday morning before a church in a typical town. He listened carefully as the bell began to peal. The sound was familiar. It was unlike any other he had heard, save that bell which pealed in the memory of his childhood days. Yes, it was the same bell. Its ring was true. His eyes filled with tears. His heart rejoiced in gladness. His soul overflowed with gratitude. The young man dropped to his knees, looked upward beyond the bell tower— even toward heaven—and in a prayer of gratitude whispered, "Thanks be to God. I'm home."

Like the peal of a remembered bell will be the truth of the gospel of Jesus Christ to the soul of him who earnestly seeks. Many of you have traveled long in a personal quest for that which rings true. The Church of Jesus Christ of Latter-day Saints sends forth to you an earnest appeal. Open your doors to the missionaries. Open your minds to the word of God. Open your hearts, even your very souls, to the sound of that still, small voice which testifies of truth. As the prophet Isaiah promised: "Thine ears shall hear a word . . . saying, This is the way, walk ye in it." (Isaiah 30:21.) Then, like the boy of whom I've spoken, you too will, on bended knee, say to your God and mine, "I'm home!"

3

*T*he Spirit of Youth

This is the "era of youth," the "now generation," a time for discovery, even a period of achievement. In today's world, the accent is on youth. Everyone wants to look young, feel young, and be young. No one prefers middle age—not to speak of the sunset years. Indeed, vast sums of money are expended each year for products that people hope will restore the youthful look. Well might we ask ourselves, Is the search for youth new to our day, our generation? We need but to thumb through the pages of history to discover our answer.

Centuries ago in that great age of exploration, expeditions were outfitted and ships containing confident and adventurous crews set sail upon uncharted seas in search of a literal "fountain of youth." The legend of the day rumored that somewhere in the great beyond was a magical fountain containing the purest of water. All one had to do to regain the vibrancy of youth and to perpetuate this vigor was to drink deeply of the flowing water from this fountain.

Ponce de Leon, who sailed with Columbus, made subsequent voyages of exploration in full trust of the legend that this youthful elixir could be found somewhere among the Bahama Islands. His efforts, like those of many others, yielded no such discovery. For in the divine plan of our God, we enter mortal existence and taste of youth but once.

However, there is a way to retain the *spirit* of youth. To retain the spirit of youth, one must serve youth. As Samuel Ullman described:

> *Youth is not a time of life; it is a state of mind.*
> *We grow old only by deserting our ideals.*
> *You are as young as your faith, as old as your doubt;*
> *As young as your self-confidence, as old as your fear;*
> *As young as your hope, as old as your despair.*

To leaders of youth I say: Never has the cause of youth so needed you and your faith, you and your self-confidence, you and your hope, you and your heart.

Listen to the headlines of our daily newspapers:

DRUG ABUSE NAMED PUBLIC ENEMY NUMBER ONE

SEXUAL RESTRAINT DOWN

PORNOGRAPHY IN THE OPEN

YOUTH GETS LIFE

CRIME AMONG YOUNG REACHES ALL-TIME HIGH

Day after day, week after week, such headlines dominate the scene. Nor may we assume that our own precious youth are safe from such sins. Many for whom we have responsibility are caught in the current of popular opinion. Some are torn by the tide of turbulent times. Yet others are drawn down and drowned in the whirlpool of sin.

This need not be. We have the program. We have the people. We have the power. Let us, each one, respond willingly to the challenge of his individual calling. Let us heed the cry for help. Let us answer the call of duty.

Leadership is more than a word when we remember that the power to lead is also the power to mislead, and the power to mislead is the power to destroy.

Our mission is more than meetings. Our service is to save souls. May I suggest five helpful guidelines:

1. *Take time to think*. Ours is the responsibility to know the program, to know our youth, to understand their dreams, to plan proper objectives, and to determine a course whereby such may be achieved. This requires thought. Take time to think.

2. *Make room for faith*. The prophet Isaiah declared that man's ways are not God's ways. (Isaiah 55:8.) The programs designed by men and placed into operation by well-intentioned persons in every community of our land simply will not suffice. For "except the Lord build the house, they labour in vain that build it." (Psalm 127:1.) Do we have the wisdom to take the Lord as our partner? He speaks to you and to me: "Behold, I stand at the door, and knock: if any man hear my voice, and open the door, I will come in to him." (Revelation 3:20.)

Some years ago one of my responsibilities in a stake presidency was to assist in the direction of youth activities. Our Young Women's president was among the finest and most capable in all of the Church. Yet, after five successful years in her calling, discouragement crept into her life. As we were in a transient area, the constant turnover of officers and teachers began to take its toll. A release from service was requested.

Before effecting the change, I felt impressed to visit at her home. It was a summer evening. She and her husband suggested the many reasons why a change would be desirable. Then came the impression to pray. Together we knelt beside the sofa and talked to God. This was not a short prayer. This was communion with the Almighty.

As we arose from our knees, eyes were moist, words would not come; but heart spoke to heart. This leader continued for many more years in her calling. She served with distinction, with devotion. We had remembered to make room for faith.

3. *Stand firm for truth*. The shifting sands of popular

opinion, the power of the peer group, in all too many instances become an irresistible magnet drawing downward to destruction the precious sons and daughters of God. Our leaders of youth become the stable force, the port of safety in the storm-tossed seas, the watchman on the tower, even the guide at the crossroads. Youth looks to us. How do we stand? May we answer:

> *Firm as the mountains around us,*
> *Stalwart and brave we stand*
> *On the rock our fathers planted*
> *For us in this goodly land—*

—even "the rock of honor and virtue,/Of faith in the living God." (Ruth May Fox.)

Let us remember that we cannot be wrong by doing right, and we cannot be right by doing wrong. A simple formula, yet a profound truth. Youth needs fewer critics and more models. Stand firm for truth.

4. *Reach out to help.* The three-act play, the roadshow, the game of basketball, the Scout encampment, the youth conference provide such opportunities. At a typical youth conference, the closing session was a testimony meeting. I made personal note of the comments made by representative youth. One young lady, in bearing her testimony, said, "I want to be like my bishop's wife." A young man declared, "This conference has been the most fun I've ever had. Never have I seen so many Mormon girls."

In a more serious vein, a young man of priest age revealed: "This gospel has brought to me real joy. Last year I baptized my father. This month he will ordain me an elder."

Many testified: "Before I came to this conference I could only say that I felt the gospel was true. After attending the conference, I am able to bear my testimony that I know the gospel is true."

Was the planning, the worry, the expense, the challenge of the youth conference worth it? For our answer we turn to the word of God: "Remember the worth of souls is great in the sight of God." (D&C 18:10.) Reach out to help.

5. *Provide place for prayer.* In the frantic pace of life today, provide place for prayer. Our task is larger than ourselves. We need God's divine help. I testify that His help is but a prayer away.

Some time ago I attended the annual meetings of the Boy Scouts of America. I took with me several copies of the *New Era*, that I might share, with officials of Scouting, this excellent publication. As I opened the package, I found that my secretary, for no accountable reason, had given me two extra copies of an issue that featured temple marriage. I left the two copies in the hotel room, and, as planned, distributed the other copies.

On the final day of the conference, I had no desire to attend the scheduled luncheon but felt compelled to return to my room. As I entered, the telephone was ringing. The caller introduced herself as Sister Knotts. She asked if I could provide a blessing for her ten-year-old daughter. I agreed readily, and she indicated that she, her daughter, her husband, and her son would come immediately to my hotel room. As I waited, I prayed for help. The applause of the convention was replaced by the peace of prayer.

Then came the knock at the door and the privilege of meeting a choice Latter-day Saint family. Ten-year-old Deanna walked with the aid of crutches. Cancer had required the amputation of her left leg. Her clothing was clean, her countenance was radiant, her trust in God unwavering. A blessing was provided. Mother and son knelt by the side of the bed, while the father and I placed our hands on tiny Deanna. We were directed by the Spirit of God. We were humbled by its power. I felt the tears course down my cheeks and tumble upon my hands as they rested on the head of that beautiful child of God. I spoke of eternal ordinances and family exaltation. The Lord prompted me to urge this family to enter the Holy Temple of God. At the conclusion of the blessing I learned that such a temple visit was planned for that very summer. Questions pertaining to the temple were asked. I heard no heavenly voices, nor did I see a vision. Yet there came to me a certain statement, "Refer to the *New Era*." I looked toward the dresser, and there were the two copies of the temple issue of the *New Era*. One was given to Deanna; one was provided her parents. Each was reviewed and read.

The Knotts family said farewell, and once again the room was still. A prayer of gratitude came easily. Once more the resolve to provide place for prayer.

Today when I think of Deanna I recall the words of Longfellow. They apply to her and to every young man and every young woman whom we serve:

How beautiful is youth; how bright it gleams,
With its illusions, aspirations, dreams.
Book of beginnings, story without end;
Each maid a heroine, and each man a friend.

May God help us, each one, as we

—*Take time to think;*

—*Make room for faith;*

—*Stand firm for truth;*

—*Reach out to help;*

—*Provide place for prayer.*

4

The Prayer of Faith

Most of the children in The Church of Jesus Christ of Latter-day Saints enjoy the privilege of meeting once each week with others of similar age and interests in the meetings of Primary. There are, however, other children, equally as sweet and precious, who are not so fortunate.

Some years ago while visiting in Australia, I accompanied the mission president on a flight to Darwin to break ground for that city's first Latter-day Saint chapel. We stopped for refueling at the small mining community of Mt. Isa. There we were met at the terminal by a mother and her two children of Primary age. She introduced herself as Judith Louden and mentioned that she and her two children were the only members of the Church in the town. Her husband, Richard, was not a member. After four years as Church members they had never lived where there was an organized branch of the Church. We held a brief meeting, where I discussed the importance of holding a Home Primary session each week. I promised to send from Church headquarters the Home Primary materials to assist them. There was a commitment to pray, to meet, to persevere in faith.

Upon returning to Salt Lake City, I not only sent the promised materials, but also a subscription to the *Friend*.

Years later, while attending the stake conference of the

Brisbane Australia Stake, I mentioned in a priesthood session the plight of this faithful woman and her children. I said, "Someday I hope to learn how that Home Primary succeeded and to meet the nonmember husband and father of that choice family." One of the brethren in the meeting stood and said, "Brother Monson, I am Richard Louden, the husband of that good woman and father of those precious children. Prayer and Primary brought me into the Church."

The power of prayer again came to mind recently. I was on assignment in the beautiful city of Buenos Aires, Argentina. The sun was bright and cheerful. Its warmth was a welcome reprieve from the winter's cold I had left at home.

I paused by the historic Palermo Park, which graces the downtown area, and realized that this was sacred ground, for here on Christmas Day in 1925 Elder Melvin J. Ballard, an apostle of the Lord, dedicated all of South America for the preaching of the gospel. What a fulfillment to an inspired prayer is evident today as the growth of the Church in that land exceeds all expectations!

In that same park is a large statue of George Washington, the father of the United States and its first president. As I gazed at the statue, my thoughts returned to the cold of Pennsylvania, to another historic place where prayer played a vital role—even Valley Forge. It was there that this same Washington led his badly battered, ill-fed, and scantily clad troops to winter quarters.

Today, in a quiet grove at Valley Forge, there is a heroic-sized monument to Washington. He is depicted not astride a charging horse nor overlooking a battlefield of glory, but kneeling in humble prayer, calling upon the God of Heaven for divine help. To gaze upon the statue prompts the mind to remember the oft-heard expression, "A man stands tallest when upon his knees."

Men and women of integrity, character, and purpose

have ever recognized a power higher than themselves and have sought through prayer to be guided by such power. Such has it ever been. So shall it ever be.

From the very beginning, Father Adam was commanded to "call upon God in the name of the Son forevermore." (Moses 5:8.) Adam prayed. Abraham prayed. Moses prayed, and so did every prophet pray to that God whence came his strength. Like the sands slipping through an hourglass, generations of mankind were born, lived, and then died. At long last came that glorious event for which prophets prayed, psalmists sang, martyrs died, and mankind hoped.

The birth of the babe in Bethlehem was transcendent in its beauty and singular in its significance. Jesus of Nazareth brought prophecy to fulfillment. He cleansed lepers, He restored sight, He opened ears, He penetrated hearts, He renewed life, He taught truth, He saved all. In so doing, He honored His Father and provided you and me with an example worthy of emulation. More than any prophet or leader, He showed us how to pray. Who can fail to remember His agony in Gethsemane and that fervent prayer: "O my Father, if it be possible, let this cup pass from me: nevertheless not as I will, but as thou wilt." (Matthew 26:39.) And His injunction: "Watch and pray, that ye enter not into temptation." (Matthew 26:41.) It is then that we remember:

"When thou prayest, thou shalt not be as the hypocrites are: for they love to pray standing in the synagogues and in the corners of the streets, that they may be seen of men. . . .

"But thou, when thou prayest, . . . pray to thy Father which is in secret; and thy Father which seeth in secret shall reward thee openly.

"After this manner therefore pray ye: Our Father which art in heaven, Hallowed be thy name.

"Thy kingdom come. Thy will be done in earth, as it is in heaven.

"Give us this day our daily bread.

"And forgive us our debts, as we forgive our debtors.

"And lead us not into temptation, but deliver us from evil: For thine is the kingdom, and the power, and the glory, for ever." (Matthew 5:5-13.)

This guiding instruction has helped troubled souls discover the peace for which they fervently yearn and earnestly hope.

Unfortunately, prosperity, abundance, honor, and praise lead some men to the false security of haughty self-assurance and the abandonment of the inclination to pray. Conversely, turmoil, tribulation, sickness, and death crumble the castles of men's pride and bring them to their knees to plead for power from on High.

I suppose that during the holocaust of World War II more of the people living on this earth paused to pray than at any other time in our history. Who can count the anxious wives and children who asked for Almighty God's protecting care to be with absent husbands and fathers? Who can calculate the concern of soldiers locked in mortal combat as they prayed for loved ones so far away? Prayers are heard. Prayers are answered.

Heartwarming is the example of the mother in America who prayed for her son's well-being as the vessel on which he served sailed into the bloody cauldron known as the Pacific Theatre of War. Each morning she would arise from her knees and serve as a volunteer on those production lines which became lifelines to men in battle. Could it be that a mother's own handiwork might somehow directly affect the life of a loved one? All who knew her and her family cherished the actual account of her seaman son, Elgin Staples, whose ship went down off Guadalcanal. Staples was swept over the side; but he survived, thanks to a life belt that proved, on later examination, to have been inspected, packed, and stamped back home in Akron, Ohio, by his own mother!

I know not by what method rare,
But this I know, God answers prayer.
I know that He has given His word
That tells me prayer is always heard
And will be answered, soon or late,
And so I pray and calmly wait.

I know not if the blessing sought
Will come just in the way I thought,
But leave my prayers with Him alone,
Whose ways are wiser than my own—
Assured that He will grant my quest,
Or send some answer far more blessed.
ELIZA M. HICKOCK

Well might the younger generation ask, "But what about today? Does He still hear? Does He continue to answer?" To which I promptly reply: "There is no expiration date on the Lord's injunction to pray. As we remember Him, He will remember us."

Most of the time there are no flags waving or bands playing when prayer is answered. His miracles are frequently performed in a quiet and natural manner.

Some years ago I received the appointment to attend stake conference in Grand Junction, Colorado. As the plane circled the airport amidst heavy snow, the pilot's voice announced that it appeared our landing would not be possible, and Grand Junction would of necessity be overflown. I knew that I had been assigned to this conference by a prophet, and prayed that the weather would permit a landing. Suddenly the pilot said, "There is an opening in the cover. We'll attempt a landing." That phrase is always a bit frightening to any air traveler.

Our landing was accomplished safely, and the entire con-

27

ference went without incident. I wondered why I in particular had been assigned there. Before I left Grand Junction, the stake president asked if I would meet with a distraught mother and father who were grieving over a son's decision to leave his mission field after having just arrived there. When the conference throng had left, we knelt quietly in a private place—mother, father, stake president, and I. As I prayed in behalf of all, I could hear the muffled sobs of a sorrowing mother and disappointed father. When we arose, the father said, "Brother Monson, do you really think our Heavenly Father can alter our son's announced decision to return home before completing his mission? Why is it that now, when I am trying so hard to do what is right, my prayers are not heard?" I responded, "Where is your son serving?" He replied, "In Dusseldorf, Germany." I placed my arm around mother and father and said to them, "Your prayers have been heard and will be answered. With more than thirty-eight stake conferences being held this day attended by General Authorities, I was assigned to your stake. Of all the Brethren, I am the only one who has the assignment to meet with the missionaries in the Germany Dusseldorf Mission this very Thursday."

Their petition had been honored by the Lord. I was able to meet with their son. He responded to their pleadings. He remained and completed a highly successful mission.

Some years later I again visited the Grand Junction Stake. Again I met the same parents. Still the father had not qualified to have his large and beautiful family join mother and father in a sacred sealing ceremony, that this family might be a forever family. I suggested that if the family would earnestly pray, they could qualify. I indicated that I would be pleased to be with them on that sacred occasion in the temple of God. Mother pleaded, father strived, children urged, all prayed. The result? Let me share with you a treasured letter that their tiny son placed under Daddy's pillow on Father's Day morning.

Dad:

I love you for what you are and not for what you aren't. Why don't you stop smoking? Millions of people have . . . why can't you? It's harmful to your health, to your lungs, your heart. If you can't keep the Word of Wisdom you can't go to heaven with me, Skip, Brad, Marc, Jeff, Jeannie, Pam and their families. Us kids keep the Word of Wisdom. Why can't you? You are stronger and you are a man. Dad, I want to see you in heaven. We all do. We want to be a whole family in heaven . . . not half of one.

Dad, you and Mom ought to get two old bikes and start riding around the park every night. You are probably laughing right now, but I wouldn't be. You laugh at those old people, jogging around the park and riding bikes and walking, but they are going to outlive you. Because they are exercising their lungs, their hearts, their muscles. They are going to have the last laughs.

Come on, Dad, be a good guy—don't smoke, drink, or anything else against our religion. We want you at our graduation. If you do quit smoking and do good stuff like us, you and Mom can go with Brother Monson and get married and sealed to us in the temple.

Come on, Dad—Mom and us kids are just waiting for you. We want to live with you forever. We love you. You're the greatest Dad.

Love,
Todd

P.S. And if the rest of us wrote one of these, they'd say the same thing.

P.P.S. Mr. Newton has quit smoking. So can you. You are closer to God than Mr. Newton!

That plea, that prayer of faith, was heard and answered. A night I shall ever treasure and long remember was when this entire family assembled in a sacred room in the beautiful temple that graces Temple Square in Salt Lake City. Father was there. Mother was there. Every child was there. Ordinances, eternal in their significance, were performed.

A united prayer of gratitude brought to a close this long-awaited evening.

The Prayer of Faith

May we ever remember . . .

Prayer is the soul's sincere desire,
Uttered or unexpressed,
The motion of a hidden fire
That trembles in the breast.

Oh, thou by whom we come to God,
The Life, the Truth, the Way!
The path of prayer thyself hast trod;
Lord, teach us how to pray.

HYMNS, NO. 220

He has taught us how to pray. That each of us will learn and live this lesson is my earnest plea and sincere prayer.

5

*T*he Faith of a Child

What a truly glorious period of the year is conference time! Temple Square in Salt Lake City is the gathering place for tens of thousands who travel far, that they might hear the word of the Lord. The Tabernacle fills to overflowing. Friendly conversation is replaced by the music of the choir and the voices of those who pray and who speak. A sweet reverence fills the air. General conference commences.

As a speaker, it is a humbling experience to gaze on friendly faces and to appreciate the faith and devotion to the truth they represent.

On one occasion as I stood to address a conference congregation, I observed in the north balcony a beautiful girl of perhaps ten years. I felt impressed to speak directly to her. I began:

Sweet little one, I do not know your name or whence you have come. This, however, I do know: the innocence of your smile and the tender expression of your eyes have persuaded me to place aside for a future time the message I had prepared for this occasion. Today I shall speak especially to you.

When I was a boy your age, I too had a teacher in Sunday School. From the Bible she would read to us of Jesus, the Redeemer and the Savior of the world. One day she taught us how the little children were brought to Him, that He should put His hands on them and pray. His disciples rebuked those who brought the children. "But when Jesus saw it, he was much displeased, and said unto them, Suffer the little children to come unto me, and forbid them not: for of such is the kingdom of God." (Mark 10:14.)

That lesson has never left me. Indeed, just a few months ago I relearned its meaning and partook of its power. My teacher was the Lord. May I share with you this experience.

Far away from Salt Lake City, and some eighty miles from Shreveport, Louisiana, lives the Jack Methvin family. Mother, dad, and the boys are members of The Church of Jesus Christ of Latter-day Saints. Until just recently there was a lovely daughter who, by her presence, graced that home. Her name was Christal. She was but ten years old when death ended her earthly sojourn.

Christal liked to run and play on the spacious ranch where her family lives. She could ride horses skillfully and excelled in 4-H work, winning awards in the local and state fairs. Her future was bright, and life was wonderful. Then there was discovered on her leg an unusual lump. The specialists in New Orleans completed their diagnosis and rendered their verdict: carcinoma. The leg must be removed.

She recovered well from the surgery, lived as buoyantly as ever, and never complained. Then the doctors discovered that the cancer had spread to her tiny lungs. The Methvin family did not despair, but rather planned a flight to Salt Lake City. Christal could receive a blessing from one of the General Authorities. The Methvins knew none of the Brethren personally, so they placed before Christal a picture of all the General Authorities, and a chance selection was made. By sheer coincidence, my name was selected.

Christal never made the flight to Salt Lake City. Her condition deteriorated. The end drew nigh. But her faith did not waver. To her parents, she said, "Isn't stake conference approaching? Isn't a General Authority assigned? And why not Brother Monson? If I can't go to him, the Lord can send him to me."

Meanwhile in Salt Lake City, with no knowledge of the events transpiring in Shreveport, a most unusual situation developed. For the weekend of the Shreveport Louisiana Stake conference, I had been assigned to El Paso, Texas. President Ezra Taft Benson called me to his office and explained that one of the other Brethren had done some preparatory work regarding the stake division in El Paso. He asked if I would mind were another to be assigned to El Paso and I assigned elsewhere. Of course there was no problem—anywhere would be fine with me. Then President Benson said, "Brother Monson, I feel impressed to have you visit the Shreveport Louisiana Stake." The assignment was accepted. The day came. I arrived in Shreveport.

That Saturday afternoon was filled with meetings—one with the stake presidency, one with priesthood leaders, one with the patriarch, then yet another with the general leadership of the stake. Rather apologetically, Stake President Charles F. Cagle asked if my schedule would permit me time to provide a blessing to a ten-year-old girl afflicted with cancer. Her name: Christal Methvin. I responded that, if possible, I would do so, and then inquired if she would be at the conference, or was she in a Shreveport hospital. Knowing the time was tightly scheduled, President Cagle almost whispered that Christal was confined to her home—many miles from Shreveport.

I examined the schedule of meetings for that evening and the next morning—even my return flight. There simply was no available time. An alternative suggestion came to mind. Could we not remember the little one in our public prayers at conference? Surely the Lord would understand. On this basis, we proceeded with the scheduled meetings.

When the word was communicated to the Methvin family, there was understanding but a trace of disappointment as well. Hadn't the Lord heard their prayers? Hadn't He provided that Brother Monson would come to Shreveport? Again the family prayed, asking for a final favor—that their precious Christal would realize her desire.

At the very moment the Methvin family knelt in prayer, the clock in the stake center showed the time to be 7:45. The leadership meeting had been inspirational. I was sorting my notes, preparing to step to the pulpit, when I heard a voice speak to my spirit. The message was brief, the words familiar: "Suffer the little children to come unto me, and forbid them not: for of such is the kingdom of God." (Mark 10:14.) My notes became a blur. My thoughts turned to a tiny girl in need of a blessing. The decision was made. The meeting schedule was altered. After all, people are more important than meetings. I turned to Bishop James Serra and asked that he leave the meeting and advise the Methvins.

The Methvin family had just arisen from their knees when the telephone rang and the message was relayed that early Sunday morning—the Lord's day—in a spirit of fasting and prayer, we would journey to Christal's bedside.

I shall ever remember and never forget that early-morning journey to a heaven the Methvin family calls home. I have been in hallowed places—even holy houses—but never have I felt more strongly the presence of the Lord than in the Methvin home. Christal looked so tiny, lying peacefully on such a large bed. The room was bright and cheerful. The sunshine from the east window filled the bedroom with light as the Lord filled our hearts with love.

The family surrounded Christal's bedside. I gazed down at a child who was too ill to rise—almost too weak to speak. Her illness had now rendered her sightless. So strong was the spirit that I fell to my knees, took her frail hand in mine, and said simply, "Christal, I am here." She parted her lips and whispered, "Brother Monson, I just knew you would come." I looked around the room. No one was standing. Each was on bended knee. A blessing was given. A faint smile crossed Christal's face. Her whispered "thank you" provided an appropriate benediction. Quietly, each filed from the room.

Four days later, on Thursday, as Church members in Shreveport joined their faith with the Methvin family and Christal's name was remembered in a special prayer to a kind and loving Heavenly Father, the pure spirit of Christal Methvin left its disease-ravaged body and entered the paradise of God.

For those of us who knelt that Sabbath day in a sun-filled bedroom, and particularly for Christal's mother and father as they enter daily that same room and remember how she left it, the immortal words of Eugene Field will bring back precious memories:

> The little toy dog is covered with dust,
> But sturdy and staunch he stands;
> And the little toy soldier is red with rust,
> And his musket moulds in his hands.
> Time was when the little toy dog was new,
> And the soldier was passing fair;
> And that was the time when our Little Boy Blue
> Kissed them and put them there.
>
> "Now, don't you go till I come," he said,
> "And don't you make any noise!"
> So toddling off to his trundle-bed
> He dreamt of the pretty toys.
> And as he was dreaming, an angel song
> Awakened our Little Boy Blue,—
> Oh, the years are many, the years are long,
> But the little toy friends are true!
>
> Ay, faithful to Little Boy Blue they stand,

> *Each in the same old place,*
> *Awaiting the touch of a little hand,*
> *The smile of a little face,*
> *And they wonder, as waiting these long years through,*
> *In the dust of that little chair,*
> *What has become of our Little Boy Blue*
> *Since he kissed them and put them there.*
> "LITTLE BOY BLUE"

For us there is no need to wonder or to wait. Said the Master, "I am the resurrection, and the life: he that believeth in me, though he were dead, yet shall he live: And whosoever liveth and believeth in me shall never die." (John 11:25-26.) To you, Jack and Nancy Methvin, he speaks: "Peace I leave with you, my peace I give unto you: not as the world giveth, give I unto you. Let not your heart be troubled, neither let it be afraid." (John 14:27.) And from your sweet Christal could well come the comforting expression: "I go to prepare a place for you . . . that where I am, there ye may be also." (John 14:2-3.)

To my little friend in the upper balcony, and to believers everywhere, I bear witness that Jesus of Nazareth does love little children, that He listens to your prayers and responds to them. The Master did indeed utter those words: "Suffer the little children to come unto me, and forbid them not: for of such is the kingdom of God." I know these are the words He spoke to the throng gathered on the coast of Judea by the waters of Jordan—for I have read them.

I know these are the words He spoke to an apostle on assignment in Shreveport, Louisiana—for I heard them.

To these truths I bear record.

6

My Personal Hall of Fame

On a clear winter day I was driving with a friend along the freeway that connects downtown Manhattan, New York, with suburban Westchester County. He pointed out to me several of the historic sights that abound in this area where man has indiscriminately constructed his ribbon of highway through the pathway of history.

Suddenly, like an old friend, there came into view Yankee Stadium. Here it was—the stadium of champions, the home of my boyhood heroes. Indeed, what boy has not idolized those who before cheering thousands play superbly well the game of baseball.

Since it was winter, the parking lot surrounding the stadium was deserted. Gone were the crowds, the peanut vendors, the ticket clerks. Still present were the memories of Babe Ruth, Lou Gehrig, and Joe DiMaggio. The record of their prowess and skills is forever safe—they have been elected to the prestigious Baseball Hall of Fame.

As with baseball, so with life. In the interior of our consciousness, each of us has a private Hall of Fame reserved exclusively for the real leaders who have influenced the direction of our lives. Relatively few of the many men who exercise authority over us from childhood through adult life meet our test for entry to this roll of honor. That test has very little to do with the outward trappings of power or an abundance of this world's goods. The leaders whom we admit into this private sanctuary of our reflective meditation are usually those who set our hearts afire with devotion to the truth, who make obedience to duty seem the essence of manhood, who transform some ordinary routine occurrence so that it becomes a vista whence we see the person we aspire to be.

For a moment, perhaps each of us could be the qualifying judge through whom each Hall of Fame entry must pass. Whom would you nominate for prominent position? Whom would I? Candidates are many—competition severe.

I nominate to the Hall of Fame the name of Adam, the first man to live upon the earth. His citation is from Moses: "And Adam was obedient unto the commandments of the Lord." (Moses 5:5.) Adam qualifies.

For patient endurance there must be nominated a perfect and upright man whose name was Job. Though afflicted as no other, he declared: "My witness is in heaven, and my record is on high. My friends scorn me: but mine eye poureth out tears unto God." (Job 16:19.) "I know that my redeemer liveth." (Job 19:25.) Job qualifies.

Every Christian would nominate the man Saul, better known as Paul the apostle. His sermons are like manna to the spirit, his life of service an example to all. This fearless missionary declared to the world: "For I am not ashamed of the gospel of Christ: for it is the power of God unto salvation." (Romans 1:16.) Paul qualifies.

Then there is the man called Simon Peter. His testimony of the Christ stirs the heart. "When Jesus came into the coasts of Caesarea Philippi, he asked his disciples, saying, Whom do men say that I the Son of man am? And they said, Some say that thou art John the Baptist; some Elias, and others, Jeremias, or one of the prophets. He saith unto them, But whom say ye that I am? And Simon Peter answered, and said,

Thou art the Christ, the Son of the living God." (Matthew 16:13-16.) Peter qualifies.

Of another time and place we recall the testimony of Nephi: "I will go and do the things which the Lord hath commanded, for I know that the Lord giveth no commandments unto the children of men, save he shall prepare a way for them that they may accomplish the thing which he commandeth them." (1 Nephi 3:7.) Surely Nephi is worthy of place in the Hall of Fame.

There is yet another I choose to nominate—even the Prophet Joseph Smith. His faith, his trust, his testimony are reflected by his own words spoken as he went to Carthage Jail and martyrdom: "I am going like a lamb to the slaughter; but I am calm as a summer's morning; I have a conscience void of offense towards God, and towards all men." (D&C 135:4.) He sealed his testimony with his blood. Joseph Smith qualifies.

In our selection of heroes, let us nominate also heroines. First, that noble example of fidelity—even Ruth. Sensing the grief-stricken heart of her mother-in-law, who suffered the loss of each of her two fine sons, feeling perhaps the pangs of despair and loneliness that plagued the very soul of Naomi, Ruth uttered what has become that classic statement of loyalty: "Intreat me not to leave thee, or to return from following after thee: for whither thou goest, I will go; and where thou lodgest, I will lodge: thy people shall be my people, and thy God my God." (Ruth 1:16.) Ruth's actions demonstrated the sincerity of her words. There is place for her name in the Hall of Fame.

Shall we not name yet another, a descendant of honored Ruth? I speak of Mary of Nazareth, espoused to Joseph, destined to become the mother of the only truly perfect man to walk the earth. Her acceptance of this sacred and historic role is a hallmark of humility. "And Mary said, Behold the handmaid of the Lord; be it unto me according to thy word." (Luke 1:38.) Surely Mary qualifies.

Could we ask, What makes of these men heroes and these women heroines? I answer: Unwavering trust in an all-wise Heavenly Father and an abiding testimony concerning the mission of a divine Savior. This knowledge is like a golden thread woven through the tapestry of their lives.

Who is that King of Glory, even the Redeemer, for whom such heroes and heroines faithfully served and valiantly died? He is Jesus Christ, the Son of God, even our Savior.

His birth was foretold by prophets; angels heralded the announcement of His earthly ministry. To shepherds abiding in their fields came the glorious proclamation: "Fear not: for, behold, I bring you good tidings of great joy, which shall be to all people. For unto you is born this day in the city of David a Saviour, which is Christ the Lord." (Luke 2:11.)

This same Jesus "grew, and waxed strong in spirit, filled with wisdom: and the grace of God was upon him." (Luke 2:40.) Baptized of John in the river known as Jordan, He commenced His official ministry to men. To the sophistry of Satan, Jesus turned his back. To the duty designated by His Father, He turned His face, pledged His heart, and gave His life. And what a sinless, selfless, noble, and divine life it was! Jesus labored. Jesus loved. Jesus served. Jesus wept. Jesus healed. Jesus taught. Jesus testified. On a cruel cross, Jesus died. From a borrowed sepulchre, to eternal life Jesus came forth.

The name Jesus of Nazareth, the only name under heaven given among men whereby we must be saved, has singular place and honored distinction in our Hall of Fame.

Some may question, But what is the value of such an illustrious list of heroes, even a private Hall of Fame? I answer: When we obey as did Adam, endure as did Job, teach as did Paul, testify as did Peter, serve as did Nephi, give ourselves as did the Prophet Joseph, respond as did Ruth, honor as did Mary, and live as did Christ, we are born anew. All power becomes ours. Cast off forever is the old self, and with it defeat, despair, doubt, and disbelief. To a newness of life we come—a life of faith, hope, courage, and joy. No task looms too large. No responsibility weighs too heavily. No duty is a burden. All things become possible.

In our quest for an example, we need not necessarily look to years gone by or to lives lived long ago. Let me illustrate. Today Craig Sudbury occupies a position of prominence in Salt Lake City, but let me turn back the clock just a few years to the day he and his mother came to my office prior to Craig's departure for the Australia Melbourne Mission. Fred Sudbury, Craig's father, was noticeably absent. Twenty-five years earlier, Craig's mother had married Fred, who did not share her love for The Church of Jesus Christ of Latter-day Saints, and indeed did not belong to the Church.

Craig confided to me his deep and abiding love for his parents. He shared his innermost hope that somehow, in some way, his father would be touched by the Spirit and open his heart to the gospel of Jesus Christ. He pleaded earnestly with me for a suggestion. I prayed for inspiration concerning how such a desire might be rewarded. Such inspiration came, and I said to Craig, "Serve the Lord with all your heart. Be obedient to your sacred calling. Each week write a letter to your parents and, on occasion, write to Dad personally and let him know that you love him, and tell him why you're grateful to be his son."

He thanked me and, with his mother, departed the office. I was not to see Craig's mother for some eighteen months. She came to the office and, in sentences punctuated by tears, said to me, "It has been almost two years since Craig departed for his mission. His faithful service has qualified him for positions of responsibility in the mission field, and he has never failed in writing a letter to us each week. Recently, my husband Fred stood for the first time in a testimony meeting and said, 'All of you know that I am not a member of the Church, but something has happened to me since Craig left for his mission. His letters have touched my soul. May I share one with you? "Dear Dad, Today we taught a choice family about the plan of salvation and the blessings of exaltation in the celestial kingdom. I thought of our family. More than anything in the world, I want to be with you and with Mother in that kingdom. For me it just wouldn't be a celestial kingdom if you were not there. I'm grateful to be your son, Dad, and want you to know that I love you. Your missionary son, Craig." ' Fred then announced, 'My wife doesn't know what I plan to say. I love her and I love our son, Craig. After twenty-six years of marriage I have made my decision to become a member of the Church, for I know the gospel message is the word of God. I suppose I have known this truth for a long time, but my son's mission has moved me to action. I have made arrangements for my wife and me to meet Craig when he completes his mission. I will be his final baptism as a full-time missionary of the Lord.' "

A young missionary with unwavering faith had participated with God in a modern-day miracle. His challenge to communicate with one whom he loved had been made more difficult by the barrier of the thousands of miles that lay between him and his father. But the spirit of love spanned the vast expanse of the blue Pacific, and heart spoke to heart in divine dialogue.

No hero stood so tall as did Craig when, in far-off Australia, he stood with his father in water waist deep and, raising his right arm to the square, repeated those sacred words: "Fred Sudbury, having been commissioned by Jesus Christ, I baptize you in the name of the Father and of the Son and of the Holy Ghost."

The prayer of a mother, the faith of a father, the service of a son brought forth the miracle of God. Mother, father, son— each qualifies in a Hall of Fame.

Ringing true is the heavenly pronouncement: "I, the Lord,

am merciful and gracious unto those who fear me, and delight to honor those who serve me in righteousness and in truth unto the end. Great shall be their reward and eternal shall be their glory." (D&C 76:5-6.)

By so living, our own entry in a true and everlasting Hall of Fame will be assured.

7

*W*hich Road Will You Travel?

A ribbon of black asphalt wends its way through the mountains of northern Utah into the Valley of the Great Salt Lake, then meanders southward on its appointed course. Interstate 15 is its official name. This super-freeway carries the output of factories, the products of commerce and masses of humanity toward appointed destinations.

Several days ago, while driving to my home, I approached the entrance to Interstate 15. At the on-ramp I noticed three hitchhikers, each one of whom carried a homemade sign that announced his desired destination. One sign read "Los Angeles," while a second carried the designation "Boise." However, it was the third sign that not only caught my attention, but also caused me to reflect and ponder its message. The hitchhiker had lettered not Los Angeles, California, nor Boise, Idaho, on the cardboard sign he held aloft. Rather, his sign consisted of but one word and read simply "Anywhere."

Here was one who was content to travel in any direction, according to the whim of the driver who stopped to give him a free ride. What an enormous price to pay for such a ride! No plan. No objective. No goal. The road to anywhere is the road to nowhere, and the road to nowhere leads to dreams sacrificed, opportunities squandered, and a life unfulfilled.

Unlike the youthful hitchhiker, you and I have the God-given gift to choose the direction we go. Indeed, the apostle Paul likened life to a race with a clearly defined goal. To the saints at Corinth he urged: "Know ye not that they which run in a race run all, but one receiveth the prize? So run, that ye may obtain." (1 Corinthians 9:24.) In our zeal, let us not overlook the sage counsel from Ecclesiastes: "The race is not to the swift, nor the battle to the strong." (Ecclesiastes 9:11.) Actually, the prize belongs to him who endures to the end.

Each must ask himself the questions: Where am I going? How do I intend to get there? And what is my divine destiny?

When I reflect on the race of life, I remember another race, even from childhood days. Perhaps a shared experience from this period will assist in formulating answers to these significant and universally asked questions.

When I was about ten, my boyfriends and I would take pocketknives in hand and, from the soft wood of a willow tree, fashion small toy boats. With a triangular-shaped cotton sail in place, each would launch his crude craft in a race down the relatively turbulent waters of the Provo River. We would run along the river's bank and watch the tiny vessels sometimes bobbing violently in the swift current and at other times sailing serenely as the water deepened.

During such a race, we noted that one boat led all the rest toward the appointed finish line. Suddenly, the current carried it too close to a large whirlpool, and the boat heaved to its side and capsized. Around and around it was carried, unable to make its way back into the main current. At last it came to rest at the end of the pool, amid the flotsam and jetsam that surrounded it, held fast by the fingerlike tentacles of the grasping green moss.

The toy boats of childhood had no keel for stability, no rudder to provide direction, and no source of power. Like the hitchhiker, their destination was "Anywhere," but inevitably downstream.

We have been provided divine attributes to guide our destiny. We entered mortality not to float with the moving currents of life, but with the power to think, to reason, and to achieve. We left our heavenly home and came to earth in the purity and innocence of childhood.

Our Heavenly Father did not launch us on our eternal journey without providing the means whereby we could receive from Him God-given guidance to insure our safe return at the end of life's great race. Yes, I speak of prayer. I speak, too, of the whisperings from that still, small voice within each of us; and I do not overlook the Holy Scriptures, written by mariners who successfully sailed the seas we too must cross.

Individual effort will be required of us. What can we do to prepare? How can we assure a safe voyage?

First, we must visualize our objective. What is our purpose? The Prophet Joseph Smith counseled: "Happiness is the object and design of our existence; and will be the end thereof, if we pursue the path that leads to it; and this path is virtue, uprightness, faithfulness, holiness, and keeping all the commandments of God." (*Teachings of the Prophet Joseph Smith*, pp. 255-56.) In this one sentence we are provided not only a well-defined goal, but also the way we might achieve it.

Second, we must make continuous effort. Have you noticed that many of the most cherished of God's dealings with His children have been when they were engaged in a proper activity? The visit of the Master to His disciples *on the way* to Emmaus, the good Samaritan *on the road* to Jericho, even Nephi *on his return* to Jerusalem, and Father Lehi *en route* to the precious land of promise. Let us not overlook Joseph Smith *on the way* to Carthage, and Brigham Young *on the vast plains* to the valley home of the Saints.

Third, we must not detour from our determined course. In our journey we will encounter forks and turnings in the road. There will be the inevitable trials of our faith and the temptations of our times. We simply cannot afford the luxury of a detour, for certain detours lead to destruction and spiritual death. Let us avoid the moral quicksands that threaten on every side, the whirlpools of sin, and the crosscurrents of uninspired philosophies. That clever pied piper called Lucifer still plays his lilting melody and attracts the unsuspecting away from the safety of their chosen pathway, away from the counsel of loving parents, away from the security of God's teachings. His tune is ever so old, his words ever so sweet. His price is everlasting. He seeks not the refuse of humanity, but the very elect of God. King David listened, then followed, then fell. But then so did Cain in an earlier era, and Judas Iscariot in a later one.

Fourth, to gain the prize, we must be willing to pay the price. The apprentice does not become the master craftsman until he has qualified. The lawyer does not practice until he has passed the bar. The doctor does not attend our needs until internship has been completed.

> *You are the fellow that has to decide*
> *Whether you'll do it or toss it aside. . . .*
> *Whether you'll seek the goal that's afar*
> *Or just be contented to stay where you are.*
> EDGAR A. GUEST, "YOU"

Let us remember how Saul the persecutor became Paul the proselyter, how Peter the fisherman became the apostle of spiritual power.

Our example in the race of life could well be our Elder Brother, even the Lord. As a small boy, He provided a watchword: "Wist ye not that I must be about my Father's business?" (Luke 2:49.) As a grown man He taught by example compassion, love, obedience, sacrifice, and devotion. To you and to me His summons is still the same: "Come, follow me."

One who listened and who followed was the Mormon

missionary Randall Ellsworth, about whom you may have read in your daily newspaper or watched on the television set in your home.

While serving in Guatemala as a missionary for The Church of Jesus Christ of Latter-day Saints, Randall Ellsworth survived a devastating earthquake, which hurled a beam down on his back, paralyzing his legs and severely damaging his kidneys. He was the only American injured in the quake, which claimed the lives of some eighteen thousand persons.

After receiving emergency medical treatment, he was flown to a large hospital near his home in Rockville, Maryland. While Randall was confined there, a television newscaster conducted with him an interview that I witnessed through the miracle of television. The reporter asked, "Can you walk?" The answer, "Not yet, but I will." "Do you think you will be able to complete your mission?" Came the reply, "Others think not, but I will." With microphone in hand, the reporter continued, "I understand you have received a special letter containing a get-well message from none other than the President of the United States." "Yes," replied Randall, "I am very grateful to the President for his thoughtfulness; but I received another letter, not from the president of my country, but from the president of my church—The Church of Jesus Christ of Latter-day Saints—even President Spencer W. Kimball. This I cherish. With him praying for me, and the prayers of my family, my friends, and my missionary companions, I will return to Guatemala. The Lord wanted me to preach the gospel there for two years, and that's what I intend to do."

I turned to my wife and commented, "He surely must not know the extent of his injuries. Our official medical reports would not permit us to expect such a return to Guatemala."

How grateful am I that the day of faith and the age of miracles are not past history but continue with us even now.

The newspapers and the television cameras turned their

attention to more immediate news as the days turned to weeks and the weeks to months. The words of Rudyard Kipling describe Randall Ellsworth's situation:

> *The tumult and the shouting dies—*
> *The Captains and the Kings depart—*
> *Still stands Thine ancient sacrifice,*
> *An humble and a contrite heart.*
> *Lord God of hosts, be with us yet,*
> *Lest we forget—lest we forget!*
>
> "RECESSIONAL"

And God did not forget him who possessed a humble and a contrite heart, even Elder Randall Ellsworth. Little by little the feeling began to return. In his own words, Randall described the recovery: "The thing I did was always to keep busy, always pushing myself. In the hospital I asked to do therapy twice a day instead of just once. I wanted to walk again on my own." When the Missionary Department evaluated the medical progress Randall Ellsworth had made, word was sent to him that his return to Guatemala was authorized. Said he, "At first I was so happy I didn't know what to do. Then I went into my bedroom and I started to cry. Then I dropped to my knees and thanked my Heavenly Father."

Randall Ellsworth walked aboard the plane that carried him back to the mission to which he was called and back to the people whom he loved. Behind he left a trail of skeptics, a host of doubters, but also hundreds amazed at the power of God, the miracle of faith, and the reward of determination. Ahead lay thousands of honest, God-fearing, and earnestly seeking sons and daughters of our Heavenly Father. They shall hear His word. They shall learn His truth. They shall accept His ordinances. A modern-day Paul, who too overcame his "thorn in the flesh," had returned to teach them the truth, to lead them to life eternal.

Like Randall Ellsworth, may each of us know where he is going, be willing to make the continuous effort required to get there, avoid any detour, and be willing to pay the often very high price of faith and determination to win life's race.

At the end of our mortal journey, may we be able to echo the words of Paul: "I have fought a good fight, I have finished my course, I have kept the faith." (2 Timothy 4:7.) By so doing we shall be given that "crown of righteousness" which perisheth not, and hear the plaudit from our Eternal Judge: "Well done, thou good and faithful servant: thou hast been faithful over a few things, I will make thee ruler over many things: enter thou into the joy of thy lord." (Matthew 25:21.)

Each will then have completed his journey, not to a nebulous "Anywhere," but to his heavenly home—even eternal life in the celestial kingdom of God.

8

*L*ove the Temple, Touch the Temple,
Attend the Temple

The newly remodeled and rededicated temple at Logan, Utah, is a stately building. It prompts memories and kindles faith. My first experience regarding Logan took place when I was a boy of twelve. The Aaronic Priesthood of our ward made a trek to the Clarkston, Utah, cemetery and a visit to the grounds of the Logan Temple as we commemorated the restoration of the Aaronic Priesthood. Since that early time, I have returned frequently to these two historic sites and again have felt the reverence and awe experienced during that first visit.

At the Clarkston cemetery, most of our time was devoted to learning about Martin Harris, one of the three witnesses of the Book of Mormon, whose body rests in this peaceful cemetery. No doubt he is the cemetery's most illustrious occupant. However, I strolled beyond the granite shaft bearing Martin Harris's name and read tombstone inscriptions of others less prominent but equally as faithful. Some of the ancient tombstones contained interesting reminders, such as "We will meet again," or "Gone to a better place." One that I still remember read: "A light from our household is gone; a voice we loved is stilled. A spot is vacant in our hearts that never can be filled."

Our next stop was the temple grounds. As boys are inclined to do on a spring day, we would lie on the lawn and gaze at the temple spires, which vaulted to the blue sky, and note the silky, wispy white clouds as they hurried by. I thought of the pioneers buried in that small cemetery. As a result of the sacred ordinances performed in the holy house of God, no light need be permanently extinguished, no voice permanently stilled, no place in our heart permanently left vacant. Oh, how those early pioneers loved the temple!

May we also love the temple. One who did so was a devoted and faithful elderly Tahitian named Tahauri Hutihuti. Brother Hutihuti was a pearl diver from the island of Takaroa in the Taumotu Island group. Oh, how he longed to go to the temple of God! How he loved his wife! How he honored and loved his children! But the temple was beyond his reach. At that time there was no temple in the South Pacific. Then came the glorious news that a temple would be constructed in New Zealand. Carefully Brother Hutihuti prepared himself spiritually for that day. His wife did the same, as well as the children. When the time came that the New Zealand Temple was to be dedicated, old Tahauri reached beneath his bed and retrieved six hundred dollars—his life's savings accumulated throughout his forty years as a pearl diver—and gave all, that he might take his wife and his children to the temple of God in New Zealand. No sacrifice was too great. He loved the temple.

May I urge that each of us appreciate the significance of our temples and develop a love for them. President Spencer W. Kimball has long urged that in the bedroom of each Latter-day Saint child there grace the wall a picture of the temple. As prayers are spoken, a sermon is before that boy, that girl—a gentle reminder from mother as the picture is viewed: "Here you will marry."

Recently our two-year-old granddaughter was reciting for Sister Monson and me her vocabulary—all of it. Gleefully she pointed to a picture of a lion, then a bear, then a horse, and identified each. Can you appreciate our joy as grandparents when her tiny finger pointed to a picture of the temple, and she repeated those sacred words, "the temple"?

The late Matthew Cowley once recounted the Saturday afternoon experience of a grandfather as hand-in-hand he took his small granddaughter on a birthday visit—not to the zoo, nor to the movies, but to the temple grounds. With permission of the groundskeeper, the two walked to the large doors of the temple. He suggested that she place her hand on the sturdy wall and then on the massive door. Tenderly he said to her, "Remember that this day you touched the temple. One day you will enter this door." His gift to the little one was not candy or ice cream, but an experience far more significant and everlasting—an appreciation of the house of the Lord. She had touched the temple, and the temple had touched her.

There is no better way to let the temple touch our lives, nor to demonstrate our love for such a sacred edifice, than to attend the temple. Some years ago when I served as a bishop, a member of our high council, Brother William H. Prince, was chairman of our stake genealogy committee. I shall ever remember when he and Sister Prince came to our ward conference and spoke to us about the importance of attending the temple of God.

They indicated that for a number of years they were workers in the St. George Temple. They described how every Tuesday and Thursday, right after work, the little suitcase would be packed with their temple clothing, and to the temple mother and dad would go. One night, however, heavy rain had come to St. George, turning the red soil to red mud. As the mother, with the little bag in her hand, ran to the car, she slipped. The clasp on the bag opened, and the beautiful white temple clothing was strewn amidst the rain-drenched red soil of St. George. She rather quickly placed the clothing back in the suitcase as Brother Prince urged, "Come along, Mother. We can obtain other clothing at the temple." They hurried to the temple, not wishing to be late for their appointed session. As they came to the clothing desk, the young lady there said, "I'm surprised that you need clothing. You usually bring your own." Then Sister Prince explained what had happened. She said, "Maybe there's one article of our clothing or perhaps two that may not be covered with St. George mud, but that would be all. Let me check, and then I will know what clothing we will require." She opened the suitcase and took from the little bag the temple clothing for her and her husband. The clothing was spotlessly white. Not a trace of the St. George red soil remained on their precious temple clothing.

I learned from that message that we, when we attend the temple, can be entitled to the blessings of Almighty God.

As we love the temple, touch the temple, and attend the temple, our lives will reflect our faith. As we come to these holy houses of God, as we remember the covenants we make within, we shall be able to bear every trial and overcome each temptation. The temple provides purpose for our lives.

9

*T*he Army of the Lord

A number of years ago I was seated in the choir seats of the Assembly Hall on Temple Square. The setting was stake conference. Elder Joseph Fielding Smith and Elder Alma Sonne had been assigned to reorganize our stake presidency. The Aaronic Priesthood, including members of bishoprics, were providing the music for the conference. Those of us who served as bishops were singing along with our young men. As we concluded singing our first selection, Brother Smith stepped to the pulpit and announced the names of the new stake presidency. I am confident the other members of the presidency had been made aware of their callings, but I had not. After reading my name, Elder Smith announced, "If Brother Monson is willing to respond to this call, we shall be pleased to hear from him now." As I stood at the pulpit and gazed out on that sea of faces, I remembered the song we had just sung. Its title was "Have Courage, My Boy, to Say No." I selected as my acceptance theme "Have Courage, My Boy, to Say Yes."

The words of a better-known hymn describe our priesthood bearers:

> *Behold! a royal army,*
> *With banner, sword and shield,*
> *Is marching forth to conquer,*

The Army of the Lord

On life's great battlefield;
Its ranks are filled with soldiers,
United, bold and strong,
Who follow their Commander,
And sing their joyful song:
Victory, victory,
Through him that redeemed us!
Victory, victory,
Through Jesus Christ our Lord!

HYMNS, NO. 7

The priesthood represents a mighty army of righteousness—even a royal army. We are led by a prophet of God. In supreme command is our Lord and Savior, Jesus Christ. Our marching orders are clear. They are concise. Matthew describes our challenge in these words from the Master: "Go ye therefore, and teach all nations, baptizing them in the name of the Father, and of the Son, and of the Holy Ghost: Teaching them to observe all things whatsoever I have commanded you: and, lo, I am with you alway, even unto the end of the world." (Matthew 28:19-20.) Did those early disciples listen to this divine command? Mark records, "And they went forth, and preached every where, the Lord working with them." (Mark 16:20.)

The command to go has not been rescinded. Rather, it has been reemphasized. What a thrilling and challenging time in which to live!

Those who hold the Aaronic Priesthood and honor it have been reserved for this special period in history. The harvest truly is great. Let there be no mistake about it; the missionary opportunity of a lifetime is theirs. The blessings of eternity await them. How might they best respond? May I suggest the cultivation of three virtues, namely—

1. *A desire to serve;*

2. *The patience to prepare;*

3. *A willingness to labor.*

By so doing, each will ever be found part of that royal army of missionaries. Let us consider, individually, each of these three virtues.

First, *a desire to serve*. Remember the qualifying statement of the Master: "Behold, the Lord requireth the heart and a willing mind." (D&C 64:34.) A latter-day minister advised: "Until willingness overflows obligation, men fight as conscripts rather than following the flag as patriots. Duty is never worthily performed until it is performed by one who would gladly do more if only he could." (Harry Emerson Fosdick.)

Isn't it appropriate that in the Church we do not call ourselves as missionaries? Isn't it wise that our parents do not call us? Rather, we are called of God by prophecy and by revelation. Each call bears the signature of the President of the Church.

It was my privilege to serve for many years with President Spencer W. Kimball when he was chairman of the Missionary Executive Committee of the Church. Those never-to-be-forgotten missionary assignment meetings were filled with inspiration and occasionally interspersed with humor. Well do I remember the recommendation form for one prospective missionary on which the bishop had written: "This young man is very close to his mother. She wonders if he might be assigned to a mission close to home in California so that she can visit him on occasion and telephone him weekly." As I read aloud this comment, I awaited from President Kimball the pronouncement of a designated assignment. I noticed a twinkle in his eye and a sweet smile on his lips as he said, without additional comment, "Assign him to the South Africa Johannesburg Mission."

Too numerous to mention are the many instances in

which a particular call proved providential. This I know—divine inspiration attends such sacred assignments. We acknowledge the truth stated so simply in the Doctrine and Covenants: "If ye have desires to serve God ye are called to the work." (D&C 4:3.)

Second, *the patience to prepare*. Preparation for a mission is not a spur-of-the-moment matter. It began before we can remember. Every class in Primary, Sunday School, seminary—each priesthood assignment—has had a larger application. Silently, almost imperceptibly, a life is molded, a career commences, a man is made.

What a challenge is the calling to be an adviser to a quorum of boys! Do our priesthood advisers really think about their opportunity? Do they ponder? Do they pray? Do they prepare? Do they prepare their boys?

As a boy of fifteen I was called to preside over a quorum of teachers. Our adviser was interested in us, and we knew it. One day he said to me, "Tom, you enjoy raising pigeons, don't you?"

I responded with a warm "Yes."

Then he proffered, "How would you like me to give you a pair of purebred Birmingham Roller pigeons?"

This time I answered, "Yes, sir!" You see, the pigeons I had were just the common variety trapped on the roof of the Grant Elementary School.

He invited me to come to his home the next evening. The next day was one of the longest in my young life. I was awaiting my adviser's return from work an hour before he arrived. He took me to his loft, which was in a small barn at the rear of his yard. As I looked at the most beautiful pigeons I had yet seen, he said, "Select any male, and I will give you a female that is different from any other pigeon in the world." I made my selection. He then placed in my hand a tiny hen. I asked what made her so different. He responded, "Look carefully, and you'll notice that she has but one eye." Sure enough, one eye was missing, a cat having done the damage. "Take them home to your loft," he counseled. "Keep them in for about ten days and then turn them out to see if they will remain at your place."

I followed his instructions. When I released them, the male pigeon strutted about the roof of the loft, then returned inside to eat. But the one-eyed female was gone in an instant. I called Harold, my adviser, and asked, "Did that one-eyed pigeon return to your loft?"

"Come on over," said he, "and we'll have a look."

As we walked from his kitchen door to the loft, my adviser commented, "Tom, you are the president of the teachers quorum." This I already knew. Then he added, "What are you going to do to activate Bob?"

I answered, "I'll have him at quorum meeting this week."

Then he reached up to a special nest and handed to me the one-eyed pigeon. "Keep her in a few days and try again." This I did, and once more she disappeared. Again the response, "Come on over, and we'll see if she returned here." Came the comment as we walked to the loft, "Congratulations on getting Bob to priesthood meeting. Now what are you and Bob going to do to activate Bill?"

"We'll have him there this week," I volunteered.

This experience was repeated over and over again. I was a grown man before I fully realized that indeed, Harold, my adviser, had given me a special pigeon—the only bird in his loft he knew would return every time she was released. It was his inspired way of having an ideal personal priesthood interview with the teachers quorum president every two weeks. I owe a lot to that one-eyed pigeon. I owe more to that quorum adviser. He had the patience to help me prepare for opportunities that lay ahead.

Third, *a willingness to labor*. Missionary work is difficult.

It taxes one's energies. It strains one's capacity. It demands one's best effort—frequently a second effort. Remember, the race goeth "not to the swift, nor the battle to the strong" (Ecclesiastes 9:11), but to him who endures to the end.

During the final phases of World War II, I turned eighteen and was ordained an elder one week before I departed for active duty with the Navy. A member of my ward bishopric was at the train station to bid me farewell. Just before train time, he placed in my hand a book titled *Missionary Handbook*. I laughed and commented, "I'm not going on a mission." He answered, "Take it anyway. It may come in handy."

It did. During basic training our company commander instructed us concerning how we might best pack our clothing in a large sea bag. He advised, "If you have a hard, rectangular object you can place in the bottom of the bag, your clothes will stay more firm." I suddenly remembered just the right rectangular object—the *Missionary Handbook*. Thus it served for twelve weeks.

The night preceding our Christmas leave our thoughts were, as always, on home. The barracks were quiet. Suddenly I became aware that my buddy in the adjoining bunk—a Mormon boy, Leland Merrill—was moaning with pain. I asked, "What's the matter, Merrill?"

He replied, "I'm sick. I'm really sick."

I advised him to go to the base dispensary, but he answered knowingly that such a course would prevent him from being home for Christmas.

The hours lengthened; his groans grew louder. Then, in desperation, he whispered, "Monson, Monson, aren't you an elder?" I acknowledged this to be so, whereupon he said, "Give me a blessing."

I became very much aware that I had never given a blessing. I had never received such a blessing, and I had never witnessed a blessing being given. My prayer to God was a plea for help. The answer came: "Look in the bottom of the sea bag." Thus, at 2 A.M. I emptied on the deck the contents of the bag. I then took to the night light that hard, rectangular object, the *Missionary Handbook*, and read how one blesses the sick. With about one hundred and twenty curious sailors looking on, I proceeded with the blessing. Before I could stow my gear, Leland Merrill was sleeping like a child.

The next morning Merrill smilingly turned to me and said, "Monson, I'm glad you hold the priesthood." His gladness was only surpassed by my gratitude.

Future missionaries, may our Heavenly Father bless you with a desire to serve, the patience to prepare, and a willingness to labor, that you and all who comprise this royal army of the Lord may merit His promise: "I will go before your face. I will be on your right hand and on your left, and my Spirit shall be in your hearts, and mine angels round about you, to bear you up." (D&C 84:88.)

10

*P*rofiles of Faith

"When Evan Stephens was conductor of the Tabernacle Choir, he was thrilled on one occasion by a sermon delivered by the late President Joseph F. Smith" on the subject of the faith of Latter-day Saint youth. "At the close of the service Professor Stephens strolled alone up City Creek Canyon, pondering the inspired words of the President. Suddenly [the inspiration of heaven] came upon him and seated upon a rock which was standing firm under the pressure of the rushing water, he wrote with a pencil" these words:

> *Shall the youth of Zion falter*
> *In defending truth and right?*
> *While the enemy assaileth,*
> *Shall we shrink or shun the fight? No!*
>
> *True to the faith that our parents have cherished,*
> *True to the truth for which martyrs have perished,*
> *To God's command, Soul, heart, and hand,*
> *Faithful and true we will ever stand.**

In that early day, I am confident that youth were faced with difficult challenges to meet and vexing problems to solve.

Hymns, no. 157; J. Spencer Cornwall, *Stories of our Mormon Hymns* (Salt Lake City: Deseret Book, 1963), p. 173.

Youth is not a time of ease nor of freedom from perplexing questions. It wasn't then, and it surely isn't today. In fact, as time passes it seems that the difficulties of youth increase in size and scope. Temptation continues to loom large on life's horizon. Accounts of violence, theft, drug abuse, and pornography blare forth from the television screen and appear constantly in most daily newspapers. Such examples blur our vision and fault our thinking. Soon assumptions become generally accepted opinions, and all youth everywhere are categorized as "not so good as yesteryear," or "the worst generation yet."

How wrong are such opinions! How incorrect are such statements!

True, today is a new day with new trials, new troubles, and new temptations, but hundreds of thousands of Latter-day Saint youth strive constantly and serve diligently, true to the faith, as their counterparts of earlier years so nobly did. Because the contrast between good and evil is so stark, the exceptions to the prevailing trends are magnified, observed, and appreciated by decent persons throughout the world.

Let me share with you a pointed letter that came from a resident of Minnesota. It was addressed to Brigham Young University:

"Gentlemen: Beginning December 22, I made a bus trip from southern Minnesota to Florida via Des Moines and Chicago and points south. There was a large group of young men and women traveling the approximately same route from Des Moines. These fine young people were students from Brigham Young [University] going home for the holidays. They were all very polite, well-behaved, articulate young men and women. It was a pleasure to travel with them—to know them—and it gave me a new hope for the future.

"I realized that the university cannot do this. Young men and women of their caliber are the products of fine homes.

The credit is due the parents. I cannot reach the parents, so my appreciation must go to the school."

Such comments are not isolated, but rather typical, for which we are ever pleased. Our Latter-day Saint students are excellent examples of faith in action.

Another group that amazes the world and inspires faith is that army of Latter-day Saint missionaries currently serving throughout the world. All through their lives, these young men and women have prepared for and awaited that special day when a mission call is received. Fathers become justifiably proud and mothers somewhat anxious. Well do I remember the recommendation form of one missionary on which the bishop had written: "This is the most outstanding young man I have ever recommended. He has excelled in all aspects of his life. He was president of his Aaronic Priesthood quorum and an officer at his high school. He lettered in track and football. I have never recommended a more outstanding candidate. I am proud to be his father."

More generally, the bishop and the stake president write, "John is a fine young man. He has prepared for his mission physically, mentally, financially, and spiritually. He will serve gladly and with distinction wherever he is called."

One day I was with President Spencer W. Kimball as he affixed his signature to these special calls to full-time missionary service. Suddenly he noticed the call of his own grandson. He signed his name as president of the Church and then penned a personal line at the bottom that read, "I'm proud of you. Love, Grandpa."

When the call is received, the college text is closed and the scriptures are opened. Family, friends, and often a special friend are left behind. Suspended are dating, dancing, and driving, as the three Ds are exchanged for the three Ts—tracting, teaching, and testifying.

Let us examine specifically several missionary profiles of

faith, that we might better consider the question "Shall the youth of Zion falter?"

For a first profile, I mention José Garcia from Old Mexico. Born in poverty but nurtured in faith, José prepared for a mission call. I was present the day his recommendation was received. There appeared the statement, "Brother Garcia will serve at great sacrifice to his family, for he is the means of much of the family support. He has but one possession—a treasured stamp collection—which he is willing to sell, if necessary, to help finance his mission."

President Kimball listened attentively as this statement was read to him, and then he responded: "Have him sell his stamp collection. Such sacrifice will be to him a blessing." Then this loving prophet said, "Each month at Church headquarters we receive thousands of letters from all parts of the world. See that we save these stamps and provide them to José at the conclusion of his mission. He will have, without cost, the finest stamp collection of any young man in Mexico."

There seemed to echo from another place, another time, the experience of the Master: "And he looked up, and saw the rich men casting their gifts into the treasury. And he saw also a certain poor widow casting in thither two mites. And he said, Of a truth I say unto you, that this poor widow hath cast in more than they all." (Luke 21:1-3.) "For all they did cast in of their abundance; but she of her want did cast in all that she had, even all her living." (Mark 12:44.)

For a second profile, I turn from Mexico to a missionary at the Missionary Training Center at Provo, Utah, desperately struggling to become proficient in the German language, that he might be an effective missionary to the people of southern Germany. Each day as he opened his German grammar text, he noticed with interest and curiosity that the front cover displayed the picture of a most quaint and ancient house in

Rothenburg, West Germany. Beneath the picture, the location was given. In his heart that young man determined, "I'll visit that house and teach the truth to whoever lives within it." This he did. The result was the conversion and baptism of Sister Helma Hahn. Today she devotes much of her time speaking to tourists who come from all over the world to see her house. She delights in telling them of the blessings that the gospel of Jesus Christ has brought to her. Her house is perhaps one of the most frequently photographed houses in the entire world. No visitor leaves without hearing in simple yet earnest words her testimony of praise and gratitude. That missionary who brought to Sister Hahn the gospel remembered the sacred charge: "Go ye therefore, and teach all nations, baptizing them in the name of the Father, and of the Son, and of the Holy Ghost." (Matthew 28:19.)

Profile number three also relates to a missionary of unfaltering faith, Elder Mark Skidmore. When he received his call to Norway, he knew not one word of Norwegian—yet he realized that to teach and to testify he would need proficiency in the language of the Norwegian people. To himself he made a private vow: "I will not speak English until I have brought into the waters of baptism my first Norwegian family." He plodded. He prayed. He pleaded. He worked. After the trial of his faith came the desired blessing. He taught and baptized a choice family. He then spoke in English for the first time in six months. I met with him that same week. His expression was one of thanksgiving and gratitude. I thought of the words of Moroni, that courageous captain: "I seek not for power . . . I seek not for honor of the world, but for the glory of my God." (Alma 60:36.)

For a final profile, I mention the mother of one noble missionary son. The family lived in the harsh climate of Star Valley, Wyoming. Summer there is brief and warm, while winter is long and cold. When a fine son of nineteen said farewell to home and family, he knew on whom the burden of work would fall. Father was ill and limited. To mother came the task of milking by hand the small dairy herd that sustained the family.

While serving as a mission president, I attended a seminar for all presidents held in Salt Lake City. My wife and I were privileged to devote an evening to meeting the parents of those missionaries who served with us. Some parents were wealthy and handsomely attired. They spoke in a gracious manner. Their faith was strong. Others were less affluent, of modest means and rather shy. They, too, were proud of their special missionary and prayed and sacrificed for his welfare.

Of all the parents whom I met that evening, the best remembered was the mother from Star Valley. As she took my hand in hers I felt the large calluses that revealed the manual labor she daily performed. Almost apologetically, she attempted to excuse her rough hands, her wind-whipped face. She whispered, "Tell our son Spencer that we love him, that we're proud of him, and that we pray daily for him."

Until that night I had never seen an angel nor heard an angel speak. I never again could make that statement, for that angel mother carried with her the Spirit of Christ. She—who, with that same hand clasped in the hand of God, had walked bravely into the valley of the shadow of death to bring to this mortal life her son—had indelibly impressed my life.

Nurtured and guided by such noble mothers, missionaries match the description of Helaman's throng: "And they were all young men, and they were exceedingly valiant for courage, and also for strength and activity; but behold, this was not all—they were men who were true at all times in whatsoever thing they were entrusted. Yea, they were men of truth and soberness, for they had been taught to keep the commandments of God and to walk uprightly before him." (Alma 53:20-21.)

Such profiles prompt faith. They instill confidence. They teach truth. They testify of goodness. They help provide the answer to that question:

Shall the youth of Zion falter
In defending truth and right?
While the enemy assaileth,
Shall [they] shrink or shun the fight? No!

True to the faith that [their] parents have cherished,
True to the truth for which martyrs have perished,
To God's command, Soul, heart, and hand,
Faithful and true [they] will ever stand.

II

BE THOU AN EXAMPLE

11

I Love You

Do we understand fully the responsibility to bridge the communications gap that often separates parents from their children? The challenge is complex and varied.

For some this is the minor task of closing a narrow fissure, while for others it consists of crossing a chasm as wide as a canyon. All of us are active participants; none escapes. For the challenge to communicate is the dilemma of our age—even the opportunity of our generation.

If occasionally our generations have not been communicating on the same wavelength, and there has been too much static in the air, it seems to me that this is due not so much to a difference in years as to a fundamental difference in times.

The world has changed more in the period since World War II than in all the previous millennia of recorded history. We have witnessed a population explosion of newly independent nations, an epidemic of international conflicts, and the steadily increasing role of government in society. We have observed the first glimpses of man's ultimate control over his environment: the unleashing of thermonuclear forces, the extension of the electron to virtually every human activity, the exploratory probings into the secrets of life, the reaching out to the moon and planets.

I Love You

We have observed in recent years the accelerating erosion of many of the restraints upon human conduct that have guided the lives of past generations. There are those who declare chastity to be a state of mind rather than a physical condition. Integrity, which was once a fixed and absolute quality, has taken on a new flexibility; some seem to have accepted as their philosophy Oscar Wilde's dictum that the best way to get rid of temptation is to give in to it.

In such turbulent times, when falsehood is embraced and truth is scorned, do we have the wisdom to turn from the way of the world and follow safely the steps of the Savior? Our period of history is identified by global travel, interplanetary exploration, and international cooperation; yet we need to be reminded that communication, like charity, begins at home.

WHAT IS HOME?

A roof to keep out the rain. Four walls to keep out the wind.
Floors to keep out the cold. Yes, but home is more than that:
It is the laugh of a baby, the song of a mother, the strength of a father,
Warmth of loving hearts, light from happy eyes, kindness, loyalty,
    comradeship.

Home is the first school, and the first church for young ones;
Where they learn what is right, what is good, and what is kind.
Where they go for comfort when they are hurt or sick,
    Where joy is shared and sorrow eased.
Where fathers and mothers are respected and loved.
Where children are wanted.
Where money is not so important as loving kindness.
    That is Home. God bless it.

MADAME ERNESTINE SCHUMANN-HEINK

Unfortunately, some homes have leaky roofs and drafty windows. Healthy families don't stay healthy when the rains of sin and the winds of temptation are thus permitted to enter.

Recently an anonymous questionnaire was given to one

thousand high school sophomores. Two of the questions asked were:

1. *Do you love your parents?*

2. *Do you respect your parents?*

Ninety-three percent checked "yes" to the first question. Only fifty-one percent checked "yes" to the second question. The students were asked, "Can you help us to understand this difference between ninety-three percent and fifty-one percent?"

One girl's response covers most of the answers: "Sure, I love my parents. They mean well, but . . . when I was in a social club at school, I came home one day and told my mother that our club was going to have its overnight party at our house. Mother turned pale. I told her that chaperones were no longer 'in,' and she turned paler. I hoped she would say, 'No, you aren't' and get me out of it, because I didn't have the courage to say no to the others. But no; she called the parents of the other girls and asked them what she should do. They wanted us girls to be popular. They didn't want to seem 'kooks' to others. They decided, 'Let's say yes this time.' In short, my mother discovered her values—and mine—by a telephone survey."

As Latter-day Saints, we need not turn to telephone surveys to determine our decisions. From the Holy Scriptures there rings in our ears: "They shall also teach their children to pray, and to walk uprightly before the Lord." (D&C 68:28.) "Be thou an example of the believers." (1 Timothy 4:12.) "Live together in love." (D&C 42:45.) "Pray in your families unto the Father, always in my name, that your wives and your children may be blessed." (3 Nephi 18:21.)

When we listen carefully and obey fully we come to appreciate that the fabric of family strength is woven with the durable fibers of revealed truth and abiding love. Truth and love are two of the most powerful principles in the world, and when they are found together, modern miracles occur. To illustrate, may I turn to family situations.

First, may I introduce to you the Jacobsen family. Turn back the clock of time fifteen years. Gentle, soft-spoken "Mother Jacobsen" had passed away. She left to her stalwart sons and lovely daughters no fortune of finance, but rather a heritage of wealth in example, in sacrifice, in obedience.

The funeral eulogies had been spoken. The sad trek to the cemetery had been made. The grown family now sorted through the meager possessions the mother had left. A son, Louis, discovered a note and also a key. The note instructed: "In the corner bedroom, in the bottom drawer of the dresser, is a tiny box. It holds the treasure of my heart. This key will open the box." Another son asked, "What could Mother have of sufficient value to be placed under lock and key?" A sister commented, "Dad has been gone all these years, and Mother has had precious little of this world's goods."

The box was removed from its resting place in the dresser drawer and opened carefully with the aid of the provided key. What did it contain? No money, no deed, no precious rings or valuable jewels. Louis took from the box a faded photograph of his father. It contained the penned message, "My dear husband and I were sealed together for time and all eternity in the House of the Lord, at Salt Lake City, December 12, 1891." Next there emerged an individual photo of each child which contained his name and birth date. Finally, Louis held to the light a home-made valentine. In crude, childlike penmanship, which he recognized as his own, Louis read the words he had written sixty years before: "Dear Mother, I love you." Hearts were tender, voices soft, eyes moist. Mother's treasure was her eternal family. Its strength rested on the bedrock foundation of "I love you."

Second, may we look in on the Stauffer family. Perhaps if

we glimpse yesterday's turmoil we can better appreciate to-day's tranquillity. Ross Stauffer, age sixty-one, had little time for God. Business affairs dominated his life. Oh, in his youth he had been active in the Church—even ordained an elder. Only occasionally did Ross remember his promise to Virginia that they would one day enter the temple.

Two splendid children had graced their home—a boy and a girl. Robert and Barbara followed their mother's example. They learned to pray, they followed God's teachings, but somehow the circle was not complete without Dad. The subject of religion became taboo as a conversation piece. When mentioned, an argument would develop, or at times Dad would simply leave the room. The dream of a united and eternal family seemed so remote. Then came a day of change. A wise and understandig bishop sensed a duty to the Stauffer family. Quietly, and without pretense, he drew Ross aside and told him of a need for his talents in the work of the Lord. "You don't need a smoking elder," was the reply.

"No," responded the bishop, "but we need you. You see, Ross, the Lord loves you and has blessed you with a choice family. This assignment will provide a way for you to demonstrate your love for Him."

Ross answered, "Don't tell Virginia and the kids, Bishop, but let me see if I can straighten up."

Now Ross had a goal. It was not to be attained without effort. Fear of failure plagued him and prompted his decision to wage this personal fight without the aid of his family. He relied, however, on the help of God. Ross began to pray. He licked the tobacco habit. He commenced to pay his tithing. He accepted the assignment as assistant ward clerk.

Then came that momentous occasion in Virginia Stauffer's life. Shall we let her provide the account in her own words:

"We were attending a testimony meeting of ward officers.

Without warning, the bishop asked Ross if he would like to bear his testimony. Knowing that he had never before responded to this opportunity, I feared the outcome. Calmly he stood and almost as though the two of us were the only ones present, he turned to me and asked, 'Virginia, I want to invite you to a night out next Wednesday. I have in my hand a recommend to the temple. I've been interviewed by the stake president, and he has signed it. I love you, Virginia, and I love our children. Will you and the children come with me on Wednesday to the temple of God?' I couldn't hold back the tears. I embraced Ross and answered, 'Yes, yes, yes!' The smile on our bishop's face revealed his knowledge of this sacred secret. Friends thronged to our side. Our date became a ward excursion."

Thus ended Virginia's account. I wonder if the bishop hadn't read Edwin Markham's poem "Outwitted."

He drew a circle that shut me out—
Heretic, rebel, a thing to flout;
But love and I had the wit to win:
We drew a circle that took him in!

Which is the word? What is the key? The answer: I Love You.

"God so loved the world, that he gave his only begotten Son, that whosoever believeth in him should not perish, but have everlasting life." (John 3:16.) In what more convincing manner could our Heavenly Fathe say to us, "I love you."

Ours is the responsibility to love Him and to demonstrate by our obedience to His commandments the sincerity of our love. Then, as taught by Jesus Himself, we have the privilege to love our neighbors as ourselves. Such is the way to exaltation. Included are our families, our friends, our neighbors—yes, all of our Heavenly Father's children.

12

Great Is the Worth of Souls

A number of years ago, a very wise man, a noble ruler, King David, king of all Israel, asked a question of the Lord—and this same question has been asked time and time again down through the centuries of time. He said, as recorded in the eighth Psalm, "O Lord, . . . when I consider thy heavens, the work of thy fingers, the moon and the stars, which thou hast ordained; What is man, that thou art mindful of him?" (Psalm 8:3-4.)

"What is man, that thou art mindful of him?" The Lord Himself chose to give an answer to King David when, in the 18th section of the Doctrine and Covenants, he made a declaration that rings down through the years: "Remember the worth of souls is great in the sight of God." (D&C 18:10.)

Counted among those precious souls are today's youth. One of the greatest problems that our young people must cope with today is the feeling of being all alone, of being unwanted, feeling that no one cares, that no one loves Mary or John. The answer to that feeling and that concern can be found in a simple hymn that was sung a generation or two ago. One verse taught:

Yes, Jesus loves me; yes, Jesus loves me.
Yes, Jesus loves me. The Bible tells me so.

Our message to the world is that the Bible does tell our

young people that God, our Eternal Father, loves them; that not only the Bible, but the Book of Mormon, the Doctrine and Covenants, and the Pearl of Great Price also are testimonies to the youth of this great church that Jesus does love them. Jesus loves them so much that they have received from their Heavenly Father a gift that is priceless above all other gifts. That gift is known as free agency.

When our Heavenly Father instructed Adam and Eve in the Garden of Eden and pointed out the fruit of the tree of which they might not partake, He then said, as recorded in Moses: "Nevertheless, thou mayest choose for thyself, for it is given unto thee." (Moses 3:17.) Isn't that a beautiful thought? Our young people may choose for themselves, for it is given unto them by our Heavenly Father.

Young people may choose their friends; they may choose their vocations; they may choose to honor and obey God, or choose to disobey. It has been given unto them by our Heavenly Father. But with this great gift comes a great responsibility, for with the gift of choice comes the responsibility for choices. No one has more beautifully portrayed the meaning of free agency than did William Clegg in his immortal poem:

> *Know this, that every soul is free*
> *To choose his life and what he'll be,*
> *For this eternal truth is given*
> *That God will force no man to heaven.*
>
> *He'll call, persuade, direct aright,*
> *And bless with wisdom, love, and light,*
> *In nameless ways be good and kind,*
> *But never force the human mind.*

We have our free agency! For youth, this is a time of preparation, a time of foundation building, a priceless time in life.

"Time is precious, life is priceless." In building their foundations, it is important for each to build well, that the foundation of life might support the superstructure it will bear.

During the construction of the Church Office Building, I walked by the building's excavation. I looked and saw what had taken place in that excavation. I observed tons of steel and thousands of yards of concrete, all having been put into that project in the foundation, and many hundreds of thousands of skilled man hours, all for the purpose of building a foundation. When we go to such expense, and when we go to such effort to build a foundation for a lovely building, isn't it important that we go to even more effort and even greater expense, if necessary, to build a foundation for the lives of our young people? I feel confident that it is.

For youth, this is a time of preparation. Such is true with respect to life's work. Years ago when one would apply for work through a foreman or through a farmer who might own a piece of property, he would go to him and say, "I will work hard." And that foreman or that farmer would say, "Wonderful. That is just what I want. You're hired, young man." But today, that foreman or farmer has been replaced by a man known as a personnel director, and that personnel director assumes that an employee will work hard. He turns and says, "What skills do you have?" This is the question that is asked of our young people today as they enter the labor market. "What skills do you have?"

I talked to the personnel director of one large company who told me that for every job of common labor available on today's market, there are twenty-five applicants. One man receives a job; twenty-four are turned away because they do not have the skills. On the other hand, if that same person who is applying for work with this company in Salt Lake City has a college degree in a technical field, he can take his pick of any three jobs, and if he is in the top fifty percent of his class, he can take his pick of twenty-five or thirty jobs. For youth, it is important that they receive an education, so that they can qualify for their places in life.

Let me remind each of us, however, that education doesn't simply mean that we attend school. Education means that we learn to think. Henry Ford put it in words when he said, "An educated man is not one who has trained his mind to remember a few dates in history. He is one who can accomplish things. If a man cannot think, he is not an educated man, regardless of how many college degrees he may have attained. Thinking is the hardest work a man can do, which is probably the reason we have so few thinkers."

May our youth prepare for their roles in life. May they choose and prepare for a mission in their future. May they choose and prepare for marriage in the house of God. May they choose to honor father and mother. May they choose to serve the Lord in accordance with His great gift of free agency.

The Lord provided the counsel: "For behold, the Spirit of Christ is given to every man, that he may know good from evil; wherefore, I show unto you the way to judge; for every thing which inviteth to do good, and to persuade to believe in Christ, is sent forth by the power and gift of Christ; wherefore ye may know with a perfect knowledge it is of God. But whatsoever thing persuadeth men to do evil, and believe not in Christ, and deny him, and serve not God, then ye may know with a perfect knowledge it is of the devil." (Moroni 7:16-17.)

This is the key that will unlock the treasure chest of knowledge and inspiration to every young man and to every young woman. May youth of the noble birthright ever choose the Lord's way!

As parents, we have the responsibility of setting before our young people, our children, a proper example. Sometimes our children will bring to us frustrations. I know this; you know it. One housewife, after having a particularly harrowing day, exclaimed to her neighbor, "Martha, I have come to the conclusion that insanity is hereditary. We get it from our children!" And then, that evening, that same mother understood anew the truth of the statement that the most powerful combination of human emotions in the world is not called out by any grand cosmic event, nor accounts found in history books or in a novel, but merely by a parent gazing down upon a sleeping child. When a parent gazes upon a sleeping child, that parent remembers the thought: "A newborn child is a sweet new blossom of humanity, fresh fallen from God's own home to flower upon earth." These are our children. Our home is the place where we teach them. And in the great home teaching program we have as our theme the statement from the First Presidency of the Church: "The home is the basis for the righteous life, and no other institution can take its place nor fulfill its essential functions." When we put our homes in order, we put in order our lives and help also to put in order the world.

We remember the account of the little boy who came up to his father as Dad sat in the large overstuffed chair and prepared to read the sports page. He had just come home from work and was tired. Little Johnny said, "Daddy, tell me a story," as he tugged his father's pant leg. But you and I know what we tell little Johnny. Dad said, "Johnny, you run on for a little while, and after I have read the sports page you come back and then I'll tell you a story." You don't get rid of little Johnny that way. He tugged again: "Daddy, tell me a story—now."

Dad looked down at Johnny and wondered what in the world he could do to shake him just for a few minutes. Then he looked on the end table, and there was a magazine. He had an idea: on the front cover of the magazine was a picture of the world, similar to the unisphere design of the New York World's Fair. He tore the cover off that magazine and shredded it into about sixteen pieces. He handed it to little Johnny and said, "Johnny, let's play a game. You take these pieces and go in the other room and get the sticky tape and put this world together; and when you have put it together properly, I'll tell you a story."

Johnny accepted the challenge and off he ran. Dad settled back, very pleased with himself. He knew that he could now read the sports page. But only a moment had passed and here was Johnny again, tugging at his pant leg.

"Daddy," said Johnny, "I have put it together."

Dad looked down and saw those sixteen pieces, each one in its proper place; and he felt that he had a genius in the household. He turned to his son and said, "John, my boy, how did you do it?" Johnny sort of ducked his head and said, "Well, it wasn't too hard, Dad. Turn the picture of the world over." As Dad turned the magazine cover over, Johnny said, "You see, on the back of the cover is the picture of a home. I just put the home together, and the world took care of itself."

When we put our homes together, the world will largely take care of itself. Fathers, we may be the head of the home—but mothers are the heart of the home, and the heart of the home is where the pulse of the home is.

Recently as I was traveling on a plane, I read an article in a prominent ladies magazine wherein the author declared that the women of America were tired of their role as homemakers, that mothers were tired of being Joey's mother, John's wife. This image was an old-fashioned image, and the article seemed to indicate that the popular thing today was to rear our children until they are in school and then leave the responsibility of their instruction to the classroom teachers. Such was the tenor of this article.

Mothers, may I declare that your children need you. They have questions to ask. I think of the little boy just four years of age. It is a spring day, early in the morning. He is out in the garden and sees a bumblebee buzzing in the lilac blooms, or perhaps he notices the tiny ant making its tedious way across the hot pavement. In his own little childlike way he urges, "Mother, Mother, come quickly and see what I have found." Is Mother at home to answer his call?

A little ten-year-old girl, having successfully competed in a hopscotch tournament, fairly flies home from school. As she bursts into the kitchen, she shouts, "Mother, Mother, I won, I won!" Is Mother at home to share her joy?

Mothers and fathers, do we realize that we are making the pattern into which the lives of our youngsters will be cast? To teach our children, we must be close to our children, and the place to get close to them is in the home. We have a responsibility to set before them the proper example. I have never read a more scathing denunciation by the Lord than that which is found in Jacob in the Book of Mormon, wherein the Lord said: "Behold, ye have done greater iniquities than the Lamanites, our brethren. Ye have broken the hearts of your tender wives, and lost the confidence of your children, because of your bad examples before them." (Jacob 2:35.)

If our Heavenly Father would give unto us such a denunciation for a poor example, isn't it logical to assume that He would give us His approbation as we set before our children a proper example? Then we can look back as did John, when he declared: "I have no greater joy than to hear that my children walk in truth." (3 John 1:4.)

Now may I direct a thought to us as leaders, leaders of the youth of this great church. The youth will follow when leaders lead. A home-teaching theme declares: "Our central task is to produce an individual who walks uprightly before the Lord." This is our responsibility. You and I—we are not teaching Boy Scouts simply how to tie knots. We are not simply teaching Beehive girls a lesson in homemaking. We, as leaders, are teaching our boys and our girls, that they might have the strength, the knowledge, and the inspiration to make the decisions in life which will surely be theirs to make. We have a profound influence upon their lives. The poet demonstrated such when he said:

> *Who touches a boy by the Master's plan*
> *Is shaping the course of a future man;*
> *Is dealing with one who is human seed*
> *Who may be the man whom the world will need.*

We have this challenge; we have this responsibility. I read a note written by a Protestant minister, printed in a national magazine: "Try to fill posts of leadership in any church with nondrinkers and still get capable people. You just can't do it." A week later, in the "Letters to the Editor" section, a person wrote: "The pastor who made this statement must be unaware of the leaders of the Mormon Church throughout the world." I am so pleased we have this reputation—a reputation of setting before our young people the proper example.

Leaders of youth, may we choose the Lord's way! Youth, parents of youth, and leaders of youth, let us remember always that the worth of souls is great in the sight of God.

This is the answer to King David's question: "What is man that thou art mindful of him?" (Psalm 8:4.) We are the sons and daughters of God, our Eternal Father. Our thoughts, our actions, our very lives should reflect this sacred knowledge.

13

*M*eeting Today's Challenge

"In the beginning God created the heaven and the earth. . . . And God said, Let us make man in our image, after our likeness; and let them have dominion over the fish of the sea, and over the fowl of the air, and over the cattle, and over all the earth, and over every creeping thing that creepeth upon the earth. So God created man in his own image, in the image of God created he him; male and female created he them." (Genesis 1:1, 26-27.)

This is a fundamental doctrine, a foundation scripture, an eternal truth. To have been created in the image of God brings to each of us a sense of profound humility, and a very real responsibility toward our birthright.

As Church leaders we have been given the precious privilege to bring the young men and the young women of the Church to an awareness that they actually have been created in the image of God. When we succeed in this endeavor our youth will have a firm foundation upon which they may safely build their lives.

As we welcome the twelve-year-old boy or girl to the youth program of the Church, can we help but notice that keen anticipation, the divine hope, the smile of confidence that flashes to our view? Our solemn duty is more clearly defined when we realize that to our care, loving parents have entrusted their boys, their girls, that we might help them prepare for the race of life.

Parents are worried and very much concerned by the dangers and frustrations that youth the world over face daily, even hourly. With all their hearts, mothers and fathers fervently pray that you and I will be able to win the confidence of their children, merit their love, and guide them from the cunningly prepared and carefully camouflaged pitfalls that Lucifer has designed and, rather, take them by the hand and successfully lead them in their quest for eternal life.

Is there justification for this worry on the part of parents? Is the danger actually this real? Is temptation so close?

Recently, in my own neighborhood, a thirteen-year-old youth labored in shock for most of the night, suffering from acute intoxication. He had gulped down nearly half a fifth of whiskey—more than a fatal dose—in one long swallow. The boy was given the whiskey by a friend. He gulped it down as a lark.

Another account revealed that sheriff's deputies in Salt Lake County broke up two teenage parties—one in a local canyon, the other at one of the beaches. The youths had been drinking, their conduct was rowdy, their resistance to even greater sin destroyed.

An editorial from the San Francisco *Examiner* of January 18, 1965, described the conditions we face by asking the question: "What has happened to our national morals? (1) An educator speaks out in favor of free love; (2) movies sell sex as a commercial commodity; (3) book stores and cigar stands peddle pornography; (4) magazines and newspapers publish pictures and articles that flagrantly violate the bounds of good taste." The editorial continues: "Look around you. These things are happening in your America. In two decades since the end of World War II we have seen our national standards of morality lowered again and again. Today we have a higher percentage of youth in jail . . . in reformatories, on probation and in trouble than ever before. Study the statistics on illegitimate births . . . on broken marriages . . . on juvenile crimes . . . on school dropouts . . . on crimes of passion. The figures are higher than ever. And going higher. Parents, thoughtful citizens in all walks of life, are deeply disturbed. They should be, for we of the older generation are responsible. Our youngsters are no better and no worse than we were at the same age. Generally, they are wiser. But—they have more temptations than we had. They have more cars. They have more money. They have more opportunities for getting into trouble.

"We opened doors for them that were denied to us. We encouraged permissiveness. We indulged them. We granted maximum freedoms. And we asked for a minimum in respect . . . and in responsibility."

One cannot help but compare our situation today with conditions at the time of Belshazzar, the king of the Chaldeans. The prophet Daniel rebuked Belshazzar: "And thou . . . O Belshazzar, hast not humbled thine heart . . . But hast lifted up thyself against the Lord of heaven; and they have brought the vessels of his house before thee, and thou, and thy lords, thy wives, and thy concubines, have drunk wine in them; and thou hast praised the gods of silver, and gold, of brass, iron, wood, and stone, which see not, nor hear, nor know: and the God in whose hand thy breath is, and whose are all thy ways, hast thou not glorified." He then interpreted the writing on the wall: "God hath numbered thy kingdom, and finished it. . . . Thou art weighed in the balances, and art found wanting." (Daniel 5:22-23, 26-27.)

Too many of us have been screaming ever louder for more and more of the things we cannot take with us and paying less and less attention to the real sources of the very happiness we seek. We have been measuring our fellowmen more by balance sheets and less by moral standards. We have developed frightening physical power and fallen into pathetic spiritual weakness. We have become so concerned over the growth of our earning capacity that we have neglected the growth of our character.

As we view the disillusionment that engulfs countless thousands today, we are learning the hard way what an ancient prophet wrote out for us three thousand years ago: "He that loveth silver shall not be satisfied with silver; nor he that loveth abundance with increase." (Ecclesiastes 5:10.)

Yet, amidst it all, a young lady, not of our faith—a college freshman—speaks out in a "Letter to the Editor" of a prominent national magazine:

"I am old-fashioned enough to believe in God. Our generation has been exposed, through every means of communication, to major and minor fears—the little threat of not finding a mate if one does not use a certain mouthwash, or fear of non-acceptance if one does not succumb to a low moral standard because it is 'the nature of the beast.'

"Many of us accept the premises that 'You can't fight city hall,' 'Live life to its fullest now,' so 'Eat, drink and make merry'—for tomorrow we will be destroyed by nuclear war.

"I am old-fashioned enough to believe in God, to believe in the dignity and potential of His creature—man—and I am realistic, not idealistic enough to know that I am not alone in these feelings.

"Some say that, unlike other generations, we have no threat to our freedom, no cause to propagate, no mission in life—everything has been handed to us. We have not been pampered, but spiritually impoverished. I don't want to live in the poverty of affluence—and I cannot live alone." (*Look*, January 12, 1965.)

Speaking of this affluence, one youngster said: "Kids are caught between the values given them as desirable by their churches, schools, and parents on one hand and on the other the spectacle of mothers and fathers both working with great concentration to get 'things.' "

With these dangers lurking on every hand, threatening to engulf our youth, our mission and our calling as leaders become even more vital than ever before. And where might we begin?

First, I would suggest that we teach youth by our own example the importance of acquiring good habits. Bad habits can be such fatal pitfalls. First we could break them if we would, then we would break them if we could. "Ill habits," said John Dryden, "gather by unseen degrees, as brooks make rivers, and rivers run to seas." Good habits, on the other hand, are the soul's muscles; the more you use them, the stronger they grow.

Second, I plead that each of us will learn his duty and act in the office in which he is appointed in all diligence.

This is no time for "summer soldiers or sunshine patriots." For life is a sea on which the proud are humbled, the shirker is exposed, and the leader revealed. During wartime the penalty for shirkers on guard duty is most severe— sometimes death. This is because the shirker's negligence has placed human life in jeopardy. To us has been given not only the protection of human life, but even eternal life—the very destiny of those whom we serve.

Finally, I would suggest that the greatest gift, the most lasting lesson that we could provide these precious young men and women would be to aid them in their personal search for a true testimony concerning Jesus of Nazareth and the knowledge that can come to them through Him. In the words of the Prophet Joseph, "Knowledge through our Lord and Savior Jesus Christ is the grand key that unlocks the glories and mysteries of the kingdom of heaven." (*History of the Church* 5:389.)

The King of kings and Lord of lords, the Savior of mankind, extends an invitation to listening youth and wise leaders: "Come . . . learn of me; . . . and ye shall find rest unto your souls." (Matthew 11:28-29.) As we make room for the Lord in our homes and in our hearts, He will be a welcome companion and guest. He will be by our side. He will teach us the way of truth.

14

America Needs You

Recently I was a passenger on a flight that took me from the Pacific Coast across the continent to the Atlantic Ocean. At many points along the way, serenely seen through white, billowy clouds, were the fertile patchwork fields and majestic mountains of this great land. The words of Katherine Lee Bates, author of "America the Beautiful," coursed through my mind and found lodgment within my soul:

> Oh beautiful for spacious skies, for amber waves of grain,
> For purple mountain majesties above the fruited plain!
> America! America! God shed his grace on thee
> And crown thy good with brotherhood from sea to shining
> sea.

The Lord Himself gave a divine promise to the ancient inhabitants of this favored country. He said: "Behold, this is a choice land, and whatsoever nation shall possess it shall be free from bondage, and from captivity, and from all other nations under heaven, if they will but serve the God of the land, who is Jesus Christ." (Ether 2:12.)

Are we today serving the God of the land, even the Lord Jesus Christ? Do our lives conform with His teachings? Are we entitled to His divine blessings?

Headlines from America's leading newspapers, depicting

recent events, pass silently in review, that you and I may judge: "Serious Crime Registers 10% Increase in Past Year," "Violence Rocks South," "Racial Strife Hits East." Murder, rape, arson, burglary, assault, narcotics violations are all on the increase in the America of today. These are the headlines of today's newspapers.

The revered Abraham Lincoln accurately described our plight: "We have been the recipients of the choicest bounties of Heaven. We have been preserved, these many years, in peace and prosperity. We have grown in numbers, wealth, and power as no other nation has ever grown; but we have forgotten God. We have forgotten the gracious hand which preserved us in peace, and multiplied and enriched and strengthened us; and we have vainly imagined, in the deceitfulness of our hearts, that all these blessings were produced by some superior wisdom and virtue of our own. Intoxicated with unbroken success, we have become too self-sufficient to feel the necessity of redeeming and preserving grace, too proud to pray to the God that made us." (Proclamation for a National Fast Day, March 30, 1863.)

Can we extricate ourselves from this frightful condition? Is there a way out? If so, what is the way? We can solve this perplexing dilemma by adopting the counsel given by Jesus to the inquiring lawyer who asked: "Master, which is the great commandment in the law?" Jesus said unto him, "Thou shalt love the Lord thy God with all thy heart, and with all thy soul, and with all thy mind. This is the first and great commandment. And the second is like unto it, Thou shalt love thy neighbour as thyself." (Matthew 22:36-39.)

First, then, I would suggest that each American love the Lord, our God, and with our families serve Him in righteousness.

The road back to God is not nearly so steep nor is it so difficult as some would have us believe. The gentle invitation of Jesus yet beckons: "Come unto me." Paul advised, "He that cometh to God must believe that he is, and that he is a rewarder of them that diligently seek him." (Hebrews 11:6.) The channel by which we seek Him and find Him is personal and family prayer. The recognition of a power higher than man himself does not in any sense debase him; rather, it exalts him.

Divine favor will attend those who humbly seek it. If we will but realize that we have been created in the image of God, we will not find Him difficult to approach. One cannot sincerely hold this conviction without experiencing a profound new sense of strength.

By seeking God in personal and family prayer, we and our loved ones will develop the fulfillment of what the great English statesman, William H. Gladstone, described as the world's greatest need: "A living faith in a personal God." Who can evaluate the real worth of such a blessing? Such a faith will light the pathway for any honest seeker of divine truth. Wives will draw closer to their husbands, husbands will the more appreciate their wives, and children will be happy children, as children are meant to be. Children in homes blessed by prayer will not find themselves in that dreaded "Never, Never Land"—never the objects of concern, never the recipients of proper parental guidance. Our children will be taught integrity, which is primarily a matter of early training. To teach the young to love the truth above personal convenience is the basis of it. They will be taught true courage, which becomes a living and attractive virtue when it is regarded not as a willingness to die manfully, but as the determination to live decently. They will be taught honesty by habit and as a matter of course. Our children will grow physically from childhood to adulthood, and mentally from ignorance to knowledge, emotionally from insecurity to stability, and spiritually, to an abiding faith in God. Such is the power gained from loving the Lord, our God, and serving Him in righteousness.

Second, I would suggest that each American love his neighbor as himself. Before we can really love our neighbor, we must get the proper perspective of him. One man said, "I looked at my brother with the microscope of criticism, and I said, 'How coarse my brother is.' I looked at my brother with the telescope of scorn, and I said, 'How small my brother is.' Then I looked into the mirror of truth, and I said, 'How like me my brother is.' "

Paul counseled us, "Bear ye one another's burdens, and so fulfil the law of Christ." (Galatians 6:2.) No burden is heavier to bear than is sin. When we show our brother, our neighbor, the way back to God through applying the divine principle of repentance, we help him to build a new and better life.

If we are not careful, our thoughts and plans to aid others in making this a better world in which to live will remain just that—thoughts and plans. As humans we cannot really see very far ahead; we need, therefore, to take each step with all the wisdom we can muster. While sensing what lies dimly ahead, we must do confidently what lies clearly at hand. Decision is of little account unless it is followed by action.

One of the finest examples I know of helping one's neighbors is that of a prominent businessman who, at the height of his success, generously gave his prosperous business to his faithful employees and determined to devote the balance of his life to charitable service. He withdrew from the world of gold and silver and each day can now be found at a large Church welfare distribution center doing his part to relieve the suffering and need of human souls and to make America a better place to live. He is fulfilling the responsibility to "succor the weak, lift up the hands which hang down, and strengthen the feeble knees." (D&C 81:5.) He humbly declares: "This is the happiest period of my life."

The rich satisfactions that come from loving our neighbor as ourselves are not ushered in at any age to the sound of drums and trumpets, but rather the satisfactions grow upon us year by year, little by little, until at last we realize that we have reached our goal. It is achieved in individuals not by flights to the moon or to Mars, but by a body of work done so well that we can lift our heads with assurance and look unflinchingly at the universe.

One of the most famous enlistment posters of World War II was one depicting Uncle Sam pointing his long finger and directing his piercing eyes at the viewer. The words read "America Needs You." America truly does need you and me to lead out in a mighty crusade of righteousness. We can help when we love the Lord and with our families serve Him, and when we love our neighbors as ourselves.

The frightening trend toward crime, lawlessness, and violence will then be arrested. God will continue to "shed his grace on thee," America, "and crown thy good with brotherhood from sea to shining sea."

15

Strength Through Obedience

The poet captured the real significance of the search for truth when he wrote these immortal lines:

> *Yes, say, what is truth? 'Tis the brightest prize*
> *To which mortals or Gods can aspire;*
> *Go search in the depths where it glittering lies*
> *Or ascend in pursuit to the loftiest skies.*
> *'Tis an aim for the noblest desire.*
>
> *Then say, what is truth? 'Tis the last and the first,*
> *For the limits of time it steps o'er.*
> *Though the heavens depart and the earth's fountains*
>   *burst,*
> *Truth, the sum of existence, will weather the worst,*
> *Eternal, unchanged, evermore.*
>
> HYMNS, NO. 143

In a revelation given through the Prophet Joseph Smith at Kirtland, Ohio, in May of 1833, the Lord declared: "Truth is knowledge of things as they are, and as they were, and as they are to come. . . . The Spirit of truth is of God. . . . He [Jesus] received a fulness of truth, yea, even of all truth; And no man receiveth a fulness unless he keepeth his commandments. He that keepeth his commandments receiveth truth and light, until he is glorified in truth and knoweth all things." (D&C 93:24, 26-28.)

Strength Through Obedience

There is no need for you or me in this enlightened age, when the fulness of the gospel has been restored, to sail uncharted seas or travel unmarked roads in search of a "fountain of truth." For a living Heavenly Father has plotted our course and provided an unfailing map—*obedience*.

His revealed word vividly describes the blessings that obedience brings and the inevitable heartache and despair that accompany the traveler who detours along the forbidden pathways of sin and error.

To a generation steeped in the tradition of animal sacrifice, Samuel boldly declared: "To obey is better than sacrifice, and to hearken than the fat of rams." (1 Samuel 15:22.) Prophets, ancient and modern, have known the strength that comes through obedience. Think of Nephi: "I will go and do the things which the Lord hath commanded." (1 Nephi 3:7.) Or Alma's beautiful description of the strength possessed by the sons of Mosiah: "They had waxed strong in the knowledge of the truth; for they were men of a sound understanding, and they had searched the scriptures diligently, that they might know the word of God. But this is not all; they had given themselves to much prayer, and fasting; therefore they had the spirit of prophecy, and the spirit of revelation, and when they taught, they taught with power and authority of God." (Alma 17:2-3.)

President David O. McKay, in his opening message to the membership of the Church at a general conference in April 1957, stated very simply and yet so powerfully, "Keep the commandments of God." His successors have urged the same compliance.

Such was the burden of our Savior's message, when He declared: "For all who will have a blessing at my hands shall abide the law which was appointed for that blessing, and the conditions thereof, as were instituted from before the foundation of the world." (D&C 132:5.)

No one can criticize the Master's instruction. His very actions gave credence to His words. He demonstrated genuine love of God by living the perfect life; by honoring the sacred mission that was His. Never was He haughty. Never was He puffed up with pride. Never was He disloyal. Ever was He humble. Ever was He sincere. Ever was He true.

Though He was led up of the Spirit into the wilderness to be tempted by that master of deceit, even the devil; though He was physically weakened from fasting forty days and forty nights and was "an hungered"; yet when the evil one proffered Jesus the most alluring and tempting proposals, He gave to us a divine example of obedience by refusing to deviate from what He knew was right.

When faced with the agony of Gethsemane, where He endured such pain that His sweat was as it were great drops of blood falling down to the ground, He exemplified the obedient Son by saying, "Father, if thou be willing, remove this cup from me; nevertheless not my will, but thine, be done." (Luke 22:42.)

To Peter at Galilee Jesus said, "Follow me." To Philip came the same instruction, "Follow me." And to the publican, Levi, who was sitting at receipt of customs, came the beckoning call, "Follow me." Even to one who came running after him, one who had great possessions, came the words, "Follow me." And to you and to me that same voice, this same Jesus says, "Follow me." Are we willing to obey?

Obedience is a hallmark of prophets, but it should be realized that this source of strength is available to us today.

One who learned well the lesson of obedience was a kind and sincere man of humble means and circumstances. He joined the Church in Europe and, by diligently saving and sacrificing, immigrated to North America, to a new land, a strange language, different customs, but the same church under the leadership of the same Lord whom he trusted and obeyed. He became the branch president of a little flock of struggling Saints in a somewhat unfriendly city of tens of thousands. He followed the program of the Church, although numbers were few and tasks were many. He set an example for his branch membership that was truly Christlike, and they responded with a love so rarely seen.

He earned a living with his hands as a tradesman. His means were limited, but he always paid more than a tenth of his total earnings as tithing. He started a missionary fund in his little branch, and for months at a time he was the only contributor. When there were missionaries in his city he fathered and fed them, and they never left his house without some tangible donation to their work and welfare. Church members from far away who passed through his city and visited his branch always received his hospitality and the warmth of his spirit and went on their way knowing they had met an unusual man, one of the Lord's obedient servants.

Those who presided over him received his profound respect and his extra-special care. To him they were emissaries of the Lord; their wish was his command. He ministered to their physical comforts and was especially solicitous in his prayers, which were frequent, for their welfare. One Sabbath day, some visiting officials to his branch participated with him in no fewer than a dozen prayers in various meetings and visits to members. They left him at the day's end with a feeling of exhilaration and spiritual uplift that kept them joyous throughout a four-hour drive in wintry weather, and that now, after many years, warms the spirit and quickens the heart in retrospect.

Men of learning, men of experience sought out this humble, unlettered man of God, and counted themselves fortunate if they could spend an hour with him. His appearance was ordinary, his English was halting and somewhat difficult to understand, his home was unpretentious. He didn't own a car or a television; he wrote no books and preached no polished sermons and did none of the things to which the world usually pays attention. Yet the faithful beat a path to his door. Why? Because they wished to drink at his "fountain of truth." Not so much what he said as what he did; not the substance of the sermons he preached, but the strength of the life he led.

To know that a poor man consistently and cheerfully gave at least twice a tenth to the Lord gave one a clearer insight into the true meaning of tithing. To see him minister to the hungered and take in the stranger made one know that he did it as he would do so to the Master. To pray with him and partake of his confidence of divine intercession was to experience a new medium of communication.

Well could it be said he kept the first and great commandment, and the second which is like unto it, that his bowels were full of charity toward all men, that virtue garnished his thoughts unceasingly, and consequently, his confidence waxed strong in the presence of God. This man had the glow of goodness and the radiance of righteousness. His strength came from obedience.

The strength that we earnestly seek today to meet the challenges of a complex and changing world can be ours when, with fortitude and resolute courage, we stand and declare with Joshua, "As for me and my house, we will serve the Lord." (Joshua 24:15.)

16

*T*he Paths Jesus Walked

On a chilly December day, we gathered in the Salt Lake Tabernacle to pay honor and tribute to a man whom we loved, honored, and followed—even President Harold B. Lee. Prophetic in his utterance, powerful in his leadership, devoted in his service, President Lee inspired in all of us a desire to achieve perfection. He counseled us, "Keep the commandments of God. Follow the pathway of the Lord."

One day later, in a very sacred room on an upper floor of the Salt Lake Temple, his successor was chosen, sustained, and set apart to his sacred calling. Untiring in his labor, humble in his manner, inspiring in his testimony, President Spencer W. Kimball invited us to continue the course charted by President Lee. He spoke the same penetrating words: "Keep the commandments of God. Follow the pathway of the Lord. Walk in his footsteps."

Later that same evening, I happened to glance at a travel brochure that had arrived at my home several days earlier. It was printed in breathtaking color and written with persuasive skill. The reader was invited to visit the fjords of Norway and the alps of Switzerland, all in one packaged tour. Yet another offering beckoned the reader to Bethlehem—even the Holy Land—cradle of Christianity. The closing lines of the brochure's message contained the simple yet powerful appeal, "Come and walk where Jesus walked."

My thoughts turned to the counsel God's prophets—even President Lee and President Kimball—had provided: "Follow the pathway of the Lord. Walk in His footsteps." I reflected on the words penned by the poet:

I walked today where Jesus walked
In days of long ago;
I wandered down each path He knew,
With reverent step and slow.
Those little lanes, they have not changed—
A sweet peace fills the air.
I walked today where Jesus walked,
And felt His presence there.

I knelt today where Jesus knelt,
Where all alone He prayed;
The Garden of Gethsemane—
My heart felt unafraid!
I picked my heavy burden up,
And with Him by my side,
I climbed the Hill of Calvary
Where on the cross He died!

I walked today where Jesus walked
And felt Him close to me.

DANIEL S. TWOHIG

In a very real sense, all can walk where Jesus walked when, with His words on our lips, His spirit in our hearts, and His teachings in our lives, we journey through mortality. I would hope that we would walk as He walked—with confidence in the future, with an abiding faith in His Father, and with a genuine love for others.

Jesus walked the *path of disappointment*.

Can one appreciate His lament over the Holy City? "O Jerusalem, Jerusalem, which killest the prophets, and stonest them that are sent unto thee; how often would I have gathered my children together, as a hen doth gather her brood under her wings, and ye would not!" (Luke 13:34.)

Jesus walked the *path of temptation*.

That evil one, amassing his greatest strength, his most inviting sophistry, tempted Him who had fasted for forty days and forty nights and was an hungered. Came the taunt: "If thou be the Son of God, command that these stones be made bread."

The reply: "Man shall not live by bread alone." Again, "If thou be the Son of God, cast thyself down: for it is written, He shall give his angels charge concerning thee." The answer: "Thou shalt not tempt the Lord thy God." Still again: "The kingdoms of the world, and the glory of them . . . will I give thee, if thou wilt fall down and worship me." The Master replied, "Get thee hence, Satan: for it is written, Thou shalt worship the Lord thy God, and him only shalt thou serve." (Matthew 4:3-10.)

Jesus walked the *path of pain*.

Consider the agony of Gethsemane: "Father, if thou be willing, remove this cup from me: nevertheless not my will, but thine, be done. . . . And being in an agony he prayed more earnestly: and his sweat was as it were great drops of blood falling down to the ground." (Luke 22:42, 44.)

And who among us can forget the cruelty of the cross. His words: "I thirst . . . It is finished. . . ." (John 19:28, 30.)

Yes, each of us will walk the path of disappointment, perhaps due to an opportunity lost, a power misused, or a loved one not taught. The path of temptation, too, will be the path of each. "And it must needs be that the devil should tempt the children of men, or they could not be agents unto themselves." (D&C 29:39.)

Likewise shall we walk the path of pain. We cannot go to heaven in a feather bed. The Savior of the world entered after great pain and suffering. We, as servants, can expect no more than the Master. Before Easter there must be a cross.

While we walk these paths which bring forth bitter sorrow, we can also walk those paths which yield eternal joy.

We, with Jesus, can walk the *path of obedience*.

It will not be easy. "Though he were a Son, yet learned he obedience by the things which he suffered." (Hebrews 5:8.) Let our watchword be the heritage bequeathed us by Samuel: "Behold, to obey is better than sacrifice, and to hearken than the fat of rams." (1 Samuel 15:22.) Let us remember that the end result of disobedience is captivity and death, while the reward for obedience is liberty and eternal life.

We, like Jesus, can walk the *path of service*.

Like a glowing searchlight of goodness is the life of Jesus as He ministered among men. He brought strength to the limbs of the cripple, sight to the eyes of the blind, hearing to the ears of the deaf, and life to the body of the dead.

His parables preach power. With the good Samaritan He taught: "Love thy neighbour." (Luke 10:27.) Through His kindness to the woman taken in adultery, He taught compassionate understanding. In His parable of the talents, He taught each of us to improve himself and to strive for perfection. Well could He have been preparing us for our journey along His pathway.

Finally, He walked the *path of prayer*.

Three great lessons from three timeless prayers. First, from His ministry: "When ye pray, say, Our Father which art in heaven, Hallowed be thy name." (Luke 11:2.)

Second, from Gethsemane: "Not my will, but thine, be done." (Luke 22:42.)

Third, from the cross: "Father, forgive them; for they know not what they do." (Luke 23:34.)

It is by walking the path of prayer that we commune with the Father and become partakers of His power.

Shall we have the faith, even the desire, to walk these pathways that Jesus walked? God's prophet, seer, and revelator has invited us to do so. All we need do is follow him, for this is the pathway he walks.

My first acquaintance with our prophet leader was many years ago when I served as a young bishop in Salt Lake City. One morning, when I answered my telephone, a voice said, "This is Elder Spencer W. Kimball. I have a favor to ask of you. In your ward, hidden away behind a large building on Fifth South Street, is a tiny trailer home. Living there is Margaret Bird, a Navajo widow. She feels unwanted, unneeded, and lost. Could you and the Relief Society presidency seek her out, extend to her the hand of fellowship, and provide her a special welcome?" This we did.

A miracle resulted. Margaret Bird blossomed in her new-found environment. Despair disappeared. The widow in her affliction had been visited. The lost sheep had been found. Each one who participated in the simple human drama emerged a better person.

In reality, the true shepherd was the concerned apostle who, leaving the ninety and nine of his ministry, went in search of the precious soul who was lost. Spencer W. Kimball had walked the pathway Jesus walked.

As you and I walk the pathway Jesus walked, let us listen for the sound of sandaled feet. Let us reach out for the Carpenter's hand. Then we shall come to know Him. He may come to us as one unknown, without a name, as by the lakeside He came to those men who knew Him not. He speaks to us the same words, "Follow thou me," and sets us to the task which He has to fulfill for our time. He commands, and to those who obey Him, whether they be wise or simple, He will reveal Himself in the toils, the conflicts, the sufferings that they shall pass through in His fellowship; and they shall learn in their own experience who He is.

We discover He is more than the Babe in Bethlehem, more than the carpenter's son, more than the greatest teacher ever to live. We come to know Him as the Son of God. He never fashioned a statue, painted a picture, wrote a poem, or led an army. He never wore a crown or held a scepter or threw around His shoulder a purple robe. His forgiveness was unbounded, His patience inexhaustible, His courage without limit.

Jesus changed men. He changed their habits, their opinions, their ambitions. He changed their tempers, their dispositions, their natures. He changed men's hearts.

One thinks of the fisherman called Simon, better known to you and to me as Peter, chief among the apostles. Doubting, disbelieving, impetuous Peter was to remember the night when Jesus was led away to the high priest. This was the night when the throng "began to spit on [the Savior], and to cover his face, . . . to buffet him, . . . and the servants did strike him with the palms of their hands." (Mark 14:65.)

Where was Peter, who had promised to die with Him and never to deny Him? The sacred record reveals, "And Peter followed him afar off, even into the palace of the high priest: and he sat with the servants, and warmed himself at the fire." (Mark 14:54.) That was the night when Peter, in fulfillment of the Master's prophecy, did indeed deny Him thrice. Amidst the pushing, the jeers, and the blows, the Lord, in the agony of His humiliation, in the majesty of His silence, turned and looked upon Peter.

As one chronicler described the change, "It was enough. Peter knew no more danger, he feared no more death. He rushed into the night to meet the morning dawn. This broken-hearted penitent stood before the tribunal of his own conscience, and there his old life, his old shame, his old weakness, his old self was doomed to that death of godly sorrow which was to issue in a new and a nobler birth." (Frederic W.

Farrar, *The Life of Christ*, Portland, Oregon: Farrar Publications, 1964, p. 604.)

Then there was Saul of Tarsus, a scholar, familiar with the rabbinical writings in which certain modern scholars find such stores of treasure. For some reason, these writings did not reach Paul's need, and he kept on crying, "O wretched man that I am! who shall deliver me from the body of this death?" (Romans 7:24.) And then one day he met Jesus, and behold, all things became new. From that day to the day of his death, Paul urged men to "put off... the old man" and to "put on the new man, which after God is created in righteousness and true holiness." (Ephesians 4:22, 24.)

The passage of time has not altered the capacity of the Redeemer to change men's lives. As He said to the dead Lazarus, so He says to you and me: "Come forth." (John 11:43.) Come forth from the despair of doubt. Come forth from the sorrow of sin. Come forth from the death of disbelief. Come forth to a newness of life. Come forth.

As we do, and direct our footsteps along the paths that Jesus walked, let us remember the testimony Jesus gave: "Behold, I am Jesus Christ, whom the prophets testified shall come into the world. ... I am the light and ... life of the world." (3 Nephi 11:10-11.) "I am the first and the last; I am he who liveth, I am he who was slain; I am your advocate with the Father." (D&C 110:4.)

To His testimony I add my witness: He lives.

17

Successful Leadership

When a member of your bishopric stopped by your home and asked that you serve the Lord as a Scoutmaster, a teacher of a Beehive class, or perhaps a secretary or executive in the Sunday School, did you actually stop and contemplate the true meaning of your acceptance? Did you look upon your assignment in terms of twenty-four Boy Scouts, or twelve Beehive girls, or perhaps an obligation to devote two hours each Sunday morning? Or did you reflect upon the real meaning of your opportunity as the words of the Lord found lodgment in your heart: "Remember the worth of souls is great in the sight of God." (D&C 18:10.) If so, you were humbled as you became aware that God, our Eternal Father, and His Beloved Son had chosen you to play a vital role in a glorious cause. "This is my work and my glory—to bring to pass the immortality and eternal life of man." (Moses 1:39.)

It was then that you determined to become the leader whose service would be pleasing to our Heavenly Father and whose example could be implicitly followed by His precious youth as they seriously lived a game played in their boyhood and girlhood days called "Follow the Leader."

What are the traits of a successful leader? How may we recognize him? Why is he different from many others? May we consider what I have chosen to call the six identifying traits of a successful leader. These traits provide a blueprint that points the way toward success.

First, the successful leader has faith. He recognizes that the greatest force in this world today is the power of God as it works through man. He takes comfort from the very real assurance that divine help can be his blessing. He is, through his faith, a believer in prayer, knowing that prayer provides power—spiritual power, and that prayer provides peace—spiritual peace. He knows and he teaches youth that the recognition of a power higher than man himself does not in any sense debase him; rather, it exalts him. He further declares, "If we will but realize that we have been created in the image of God, we will not find Him difficult to approach." This knowledge, acquired through faith, accounts for the inner calm that characterizes the successful leader.

Second, the successful leader lives as he teaches. He is honest with others. He is honest with himself. He is honest with God. He is honest by habit and as a matter of course.

In an issue of *Nation's Business*, there appeared a comprehensive report entitled "What It Takes to Be Successful." The report was prepared by that magazine's editors after exhaustive surveys to determine those traits which, when acquired and lived, will assure a leader's success. Business leaders, educators, and consultants evaluated the qualities a leader needs most; and the final conclusion revealed that integrity, and such variations of it as honesty or moral soundness, was given first rank by virtually all participants in the survey. The leader who has integrity, who leads by example, will never suffer the scorn of disappointed youth who declare, "People are always telling us what to do but aren't doing it themselves." The apostle Paul counseled us wisely, "Be thou an example of the believers, in word, in conversation, in charity, in spirit, in faith, in purity." (1 Timothy 4:12.)

Third, the successful leader works willingly. Formula

"W" applies to him. What is Formula "W"? Simply this: Work will win when wishy-washy wishing won't. Should you be discouraged, look back carefully and honestly and you will find that your work has not been done with all your might. Victory is bound to come to him who gives all of himself to the cause he represents when there be truth in the cause. There is no place for procrastination, defined by Edward Young two centuries ago as "the thief of time."

Procrastination is really much more. It is the thief of our self-respect. It nags at us and spoils our joy. It deprives us of the fullest realization of our ambitions and hopes. But procrastination is a guest who prefers to visit the lazy, and never feels at home with the busy and diligent.

Fourth, the successful leader leads with love. You never find the successful leader scolding nor giving vent to verbal tongue lashing. Rather, he follows the counsel of President George Albert Smith, who said, "It does not pay to scold. I believe you can get people to do anything (if you can get them to do it at all) by loving them into doing it." Think back to that teacher who influenced you most, and honestly ask yourself, "Did that teacher love me and my classmates, or did she scold us?" You know the answer. Where love prevails in a class, discipline problems vanish.

Fifth, the successful leader is prepared. In his mind, he has carefully stored full information with respect to his assignment. He knows the program. He knows what is expected of him. He does not approach his assignment just hoping or wishing for success. In his heart, he has made spiritual preparation, too. He has earned, through his faithfulness, the companionship of the Holy Spirit. He has knowledge to give. He has a testimony to share.

The unprepared leader, however, will find himself drifting aimlessly on a sea of chance, with waves of failure threatening to engulf him.

Sixth, the successful leader achieves results. To begin with, he recognizes that no aim leads to no end. In short, he develops goals of accomplishment. If he be a Scoutmaster, he determines that each boy will achieve. You see such a leader at every court of honor in full uniform, his boys receiving award upon award. Their leader has taught them that we were not placed on earth to fail, but rather to succeed; that we cannot rest content with mediocrity when excellence is within our reach.

Such a leader recognizes that his attitude determines his altitude. He knows full well that nothing is as contagious as enthusiasm, unless it is a lack of enthusiasm. He carries others to accomplishment through the sheer strength of his over-whelming desire to bring success to his assignment. The leader who gets the job done is one who inspires confidence, who motivates action, and who generates enthusiasm. You will ever recognize his work—for it will be well done.

This, then, is the description—yes, the definition—of the successful leader. Neither wealth, nor fame, nor any other instrument of power can ever be more reliable in assuring his security and peace of mind than the knowledge of having inspired gratitude in another.

18

*L*eadership—Our Challenge Today

We are the sons and daughters of Almighty God. We have a destiny to fulfill, a life to live, a contribution to make, a goal to achieve. The future of our country in these rapidly changing times awaits our mark of influence. The growth of the kingdom of God upon the earth will, in part, be aided by our devotion.

We have been provided the God-given blessing of free agency. The pathway is marked. The blessings and penalties are shown clearly. But the choice is up to us. Of course there will be opposition. There always has been and always will be. That evil one, even Satan, desires that we become his followers, rather than leaders in our own right. He has evil and designing men as his agents. Together they conspire to make evil appear to be good. In a most enticing manner he cunningly invites: "This is the way to happiness—come." Yet, that still, small voice within us cautions: "Not so. This doesn't seem right."

A choice has to be made. There are no minor or insignificant decisions in our lives. Decisions determine destiny. Whether we like it or not, we are engaged in the race of our lives. At stake is eternal life—yours and mine. What will be the outcome? Will we be servants of God? Or will we be servants of sin?

May I offer for our consideration a simple formula for successful leadership and a noble life:

First, think big.

Second, prepare well.

Third, work hard.

Fourth, live right.

First, *think big.* A story is told of a banker who would walk to work each morning and, rounding the corner of the same street, would daily see a small boy with freckled face and tousled hair playing as all boys play. The banker would run his hand through the boy's head of hair and counsel, "Remember, son, think big. Think big."

This pattern was repeated over and over again. One day, however, the boy was missing, and a sign had been erected by the lad and placed on the front lawn. It read: "Dog for Sale—$50,000."

The banker muttered, "Well, I've got the boy thinking big, anyway." That night the sign was still in place, but two days later it was gone. The banker asked the boy, "Did you sell the dog?" "Yup," came the answer. "For $50,000?" asked the banker. "Yup," came the reply. "Cash?" "Not exactly," said the boy. "I had to take two $25,000 kittens in on the deal!"

When we realize that we become what we think about, then our thoughts take on added importance. We live in a world made small by the inventions of science and the exploration of space. In these days wonders are wrought and we shrug and dismiss them as commonplace. On a television screen that none could imagine not too many years ago, we have seen man climb to the heights of the universe, step into space, and walk on the thin floor of nothingness. We have seen greater strides into the mysteries of science than others have known in all history. This is not the age of minute goals, mediocre accomplishment, or shallow thought. We must think big.

We cannot restrict our thinking to today's problems alone. We have the obligation to plan for tomorrow's opportunities. We are limited only by our thoughts and personal determination to convert these thoughts to realities. Henry Ford, the industrialist, taught us, "An educated man is not one who has trained his mind to retain a few dates in history. He is one who can accomplish things. Unless a man has learned to think, he is not an educated man, regardless of how many college degrees he has after his name."

I challenge each of us to think big, and, I might add, think wisely.

Second, *prepare well*. Our noble thoughts must be part of a purposeful plan, if the dream castles we have envisioned are to become a reality. The Lord taught: "Organize yourselves; prepare every needful thing." (D&C 88:119.) A reading of the book of Genesis gives one insight into the painstaking planning undertaken by God himself.

At times the preparation period may appear dull, uninteresting, and even unnecessary. But experience continues to demonstrate that the future belongs to those who prepare for it. And if we are to become leaders, we cannot skimp on our preparation.

Patterns of living and codes of behavior during the preparation period have a way of carrying over into actual life. John Dryden warned: "Ill habits gather by unseen degrees—As brooks make rivers, rivers run to seas." First we could break them if we would. Then we would break them if we could.

Spiritual preparation is vital. Spirituality is not like a water faucet in that it can be turned off or turned on at will. Some make the fatal error of assuming that religion is for others now and perhaps someday for us. Such thinking is not based on fact or experience, for we are daily becoming what we shall be. To be prepared spiritually for leadership over-shadows all other types of preparation.

I challenge each of us to prepare well.

Third, *work hard*. A wise leader cautioned, "When you play, play hard. When you work, don't play at all." Leadership requires effort, hard work, a do-or-die philosophy.

When we speak of work as an essential ingredient of leadership, we speak also of teamwork. Getting along with others must be part of our work and service pattern, or leadership assignments will pass us by. One cannot perform all of the needed work by himself. J. C. Penney, the business leader, advised, "My definition of leadership is brief and to the point. It is simply this: Getting things done through the aid of other people. Cooperativeness is not so much learning how to get along with others as taking the kinks out of yourself so that others can get along with you."

I challenge each of us to work hard.

Fourth and finally, *live right*. Let us study the scriptures, then live their teachings. Following the Savior's guide, let us implement in our lives a set of Be Attitudes:

—*Be diligent*

—*Be dependable*

—*Be honest*

—*Be clean*

—*Be true*

—*Be obedient*

Then we can be as Jesus admonished, a light unto the world. (See Matthew 5:14.) This is true leadership: a leader in righteousness; an example of purity; a defender of truth.

We cannot compromise our principles and retain the respect of others. A simple motto to follow is to "Choose the Right." In the words of the hymn:

Choose the right! there is peace in righteous doing;
Choose the right! there's safety for the soul;
Choose the right, in all labors you're pursuing;
Let God and heaven be your goal.

HYMNS, NO. 110

To live right, we need the companionship of the Holy Spirit. It will lead us to truth. It will keep us from error. We should pray earnestly for its companionship, for that Spirit will be to our quest for leadership success as a beacon light showing the way. Doubt not the ability of God to hear and answer prayer. He guided Samuel. He strengthened David. He appeared to Joseph. He can lead us, and does.

I experienced such guidance while serving as bishop of the Sixth-Seventh Ward in Salt Lake City. I received an assignment from our stake president to supply the stake with the names of two possible stake missionaries. My counselors and I prayed about the selection and then reviewed the listing of priesthood bearers within the ward.

We had a card file, and each individual card contained the name of the head of the family. One at a time we eliminated each of the high priests and each of the elders. My comment would be, "We can't recommend John Flanders; he's our Scoutmaster," or "We would be foolish to recommend Samuel Flake; he's busy teaching the priests quorum."

Finally, we commenced the file of the seventies. I came to a card that contained the name of Richard W. Moon and said to my counselors, "We surely won't recommend him. He's the finest assistant Sunday School superintendent we've ever had." I then attempted to put the card face down on the stack, but the card would not leave my thumb and index finger. It was as though it were glued to them. I tugged at the card, but it still would not come loose. I then said to my counselors, "The Lord needs Richard W. Moon as a stake missionary more than we need him as an assistant Sunday School superintendent."

I then related the experience to our stake president, who recommended that, under the circumstances, we should go immediately to Brother Moon's house and extend to him a call to serve. We found that he was visiting his mother, who also lived within our ward. She met us at the door of her home, and I related to her the circumstances of our decision to call her son as a stake missionary. Tears welled up in her eyes, and she said, "Bishop, ever since we heard your announcement that the Church was looking for seventies who could fill missions, I have prayed that my son might be appointed. I wondered how, with his wife and tiny children, he could be a full-time missionary. Not once did I think of a stake mission. Your visit is in answer to my prayer." Richard Moon accepted the call and became a most successful stake missionary.

Jesus, our Savior and Redeemer, extends to you and to me that same invitation given to Peter, to Matthew, to Philip: "Come, follow me." Will we do so? It is the way of true leadership. May each of us think big, prepare well, work hard, and live right, thereby finding success in life.

19

*D*ecisions Determine Destiny

When I am in the presence of the youth of the Church, I think of the prophet of the Lord who called me to be a member of the Council of the Twelve, President David O. McKay. I was his last appointee to the Council, and I shall ever remember and treasure the association that I had with him and the appointment wherein he extended to me my call. As I think of President McKay, I think of one of his favorite passages from the literary giants of the world—even from Longfellow—when he described youth. He said, "How beautiful is youth; how bright it gleams, with its illusions, aspirations, dreams. Book of beginnings, story without end; each maid a heroine, each man a friend."

Surely the youth of the Church represent beauty in all of its dimensions. Wherever we as General Authorities travel, we have a mother here or a father there or a younger brother or sister ask if we will bring a greeting to a precious son or daughter, brother or sister.

Some time ago it was my responsibility to fulfill an assignment in ancient Persia, the land of Iran. After the meeting, a father came up to me and placed in my hand a little note. Its message read: "Dear Brother Monson, My son Rodney is at BYU. I love him as you know a father does. He is a quiet, sensitive young man of whom we are proud. He has seldom been thanked for doing good or being a fine young man because he is so quiet. Can you find an opportunity to express the appreciation of parents for their children far away and living right. Thanks, Rodney's father." Then he added, "P.S. You won't notice Rodney in the crowd. He will be near the back row."

Youth of today are faced with monumental decisions. The world in which they live is not a play world or a Disney world. It is a very competitive world, which will require the very best that they can bring to it and will reward them when their best efforts are put forth.

Important to remember is this solemn truth: Obedience to God's law will bring liberty and eternal life, whereas disobedience will bring captivity and death.

It has been said by one, years ago, that history turns on small hinges, and so do people's lives. Our lives will depend upon the decisions we make, for decisions determine destiny.

Even so-called small decisions have their eternal consequences. For example, the decision made by Adam and Eve—we are here as a result of that decision. Think of the decisions made by people at the time of the prophet Noah, when they laughed and they mocked and they jeered as this prophet of God erected a crude-looking vessel called an ark; but they ceased from their laughing and their jeering when the rain began to come and when the rain failed to cease. They had made a decision contrary to the purposes of God, and they paid for that decision with their very lives.

I think of the decision of Laman and Lemuel, when they were commanded to go and obtain the plates of Laban. What does the record indicate that they did? They murmured and said, "This is a hard thing which we have been commanded to do," and they decided not to obey that commandment—and they lost the blessing. But Nephi, when he received that commandment, responded with that beautiful declaration: "I will go and do the things which the Lord hath commanded," and he did; and he received the coveted prize that comes through obedience.

Think of the decision of a fourteen-year-old boy who had read that if anyone lacked wisdom, he should ask of God, "that giveth to all men liberally, and upbraideth not; and it shall be given him." (James 1:5.) He made the decision to put to the test the epistle of James. He went into the grove and he prayed. Was that a minor decision? No—that was a decision that has affected all mankind and particularly all of us who are members of The Church of Jesus Christ of Latter-day Saints.

During the thirteenth century another important decision was made when Mongol hordes came out of Mongolia, swept across the part of the world we know as Turkey and Iran, and then entered into Europe. They were at the very gates of the city of Vienna; Western Europe and its civilization looked as though all was doomed as the leader of the Mongols, Subedei, stood ready to lead his cavalry in an annihilation of Western history and Western culture. Then something happened. A messenger from Mongolia brought the news that the Great Khan, Ogedei, had died; and Subedei had to make the decision to go on and conquer Western Europe or to return for the funeral of the Great Khan. He made the decision to return, and the Mongol hordes returned to Mongolia and never again threatened Western Europe. A small decision, but oh! its consequence.

As I have read the history of World War II, I think perhaps one of the greatest decisions to be made was the one made by General Dwight D. Eisenhower and his supreme staff to invade France on the beaches of Normandy. The enemy general staff had been led to believe that the invasion would take place at Calais, and consequently had the best-trained troops situated at Calais, ready to hurl back into the ocean the landing force. This decision proved to be wrong. The force landed on the beaches of Normandy and penetrated the hedgerows; and before the assault troops of the enemy army could repel them, they were firmly entrenched beyond the beachhead, and World War II was headed toward its conclusion. A decision that determined destiny.

Each youth—indeed, all of us—has the responsibility to make vitally important decisions. Our decisions may not be to invade the coast of Normandy; they certainly will not be to ride with the Mongol hordes toward the gates of Vienna, and we will not be called upon to make quite the same decision as did the people at the time of Noah. But there are certain decisions that youth make. They are all important. Remember the observation:

Isn't it strange that princes and kings,
And clowns that caper in sawdust rings,
And common people like you and me
Are builders for eternity?

Each is given a bag of tools,
A shapeless mass, a book of rules;
And each must make, ere life is flown,
A stumbling block or a steppingstone.

R. L. SHARPE

Will youth make stepping-stones, or will they carve out for themselves stumbling blocks? Will they travel upward and onward toward the celestial kingdom of God, or pursue a course that would take them away from this coveted objective?

What are the important decisions our youth must make? First, what will be my faith. Second, whom shall I marry. And third, what will be my life's work.

First, *what will be my faith*. I feel that we should put our trust in our Heavenly Father, that each one should have the responsibility to find out for himself whether or not the gospel of Jesus Christ is true. As we read the Book of Mormon and the other standard works, as we put the teachings to the test, then we will know of the doctrine, for this is our promise, whether it be of man or whether it be of God. Sometimes that decision—What will I believe?—can have far-reaching consequences.

During the period 1959 to 1962, I had the privilege of presiding over the Canadian Mission, with headquarters in Toronto, Canada. There we had the wonderful opportunity of working with 450 of the finest young men and young women in all the world. From that particular experience, I should like to relate an account that came to Sister Monson that had far-reaching significance. One Friday she was the only person in a usually very busy mission home. The telephone rang, and the person who was on the other end of the line spoke with a Dutch accent and asked, "Is this the headquarters of the Mormon Church?" Sister Monson assured him that it was as far as Toronto was concerned, and then she said, "May I help you?" The party on the line said, "Yes. We have come from our native Holland, where we've had an opportunity to learn something about the Mormons. We'd like to know more." Sister Monson, being a good missionary, said, "We can help you." Then the gentleman who had called said, "We have chicken pox in our home; and if you could wait until the children are better, we'd love to have the missionaries call." Sister Monson said that she would arrange such, and that terminated the conversation.

Excitedly she told the two missionaries on our staff, "Here is a golden referral," and the missionaries agreed. Then, as some missionaries do, they procrastinated calling upon the family. Days went into weeks, and the weeks became several. Sister Monson would say, "Are you going to call on that Dutch family tonight, elders?" And they would respond, "Well, we're too busy tonight, but we're going to get around to it." After a few more days Sister Monson would say, "What about my

Dutch family? Are you going to call on them tonight?" Again the reply, "Well we're too busy tonight, but we're going to work it into our schedule." Finally Sister Monson said, "If you aren't going to call on the Dutch family tonight, my husband and I are going to call on them," and they replied, "We'll work it into our schedule tonight." And thus they called on a lovely family. They taught them the gospel. Each person in the family became a member of the Church. The family was the Jacob de Jager family. Brother de Jager became the president of an elders quorum. His employer, the gigantic Phillips Company, then transferred him to Mexico, where he served the Church with distinction. Later he became the counselor to several mission presidents in Holland, then a Regional Representative of the Twelve, and then a member of the First Quorum of the Seventy. Today he is serving as the executive administrator of the work in Southeast Asia.

I ask, Was it an important decision that was made on the part of the missionaries to call on the de Jagers? Was it an important decision for Sister Monson to say, "Tonight is the night or else"? Was it an important decision for the de Jagers to telephone mission headquarters in Toronto, Cananda, and say, "Could we have the missionaries come to our home?" I bear testimony that these decisions had eternal consequences, not only for the de Jagers, but for many other people as well, for here is a man who can teach the gospel in English, in Dutch, in German, in Spanish, and in Indonesian, and now is learning to preach the gospel in Chinese. I ask, What will be our faith?

Our conversation may not be as dramatic as Brother and Sister de Jager's happened to be, but to each it will be equally as vital and equally as long-lasting and equally as far-reaching. That which we believe is a very important matter. Let us weigh our responsibility to search for truth.

To youth comes a second decision: *Whom shall I marry.* May I make personal application of this question.

At a dance for the freshman class at the University of Utah, I was dancing with a girl from West High School, and a young lady from East High School danced by with her partner. Her name was Frances Johnson. I took one look and decided that there was a young lady I wanted to meet; but she danced away, and I didn't see her for three more months. Then one day, while waiting for the old streetcar at Thirteenth East and Second South streets in Salt Lake City, I looked and couldn't believe my eyes. Here was the young lady whom I had seen dancing across the floor, and she was standing with another young lady and a young man whom I remembered from grade school days. Unfortunately, I couldn't remember his name. I had a decision to make, and I thought to myself, "This decision requires courage. What should I do?" I found in my heart an appreciation of that phrase, "When the time for decision arrives, the time for preparation is past." I squared my shoulders up and plunged toward my opportunity. I walked up to the young man and said, "Hello, my old friend from grade-school days," and he said to me, "I can't remember your name." I told him my name, and he told me his name; and then he introduced me to the girl who later became my wife. That day I made a little note in my student directory to call on Frances Beverly Johnson, and I did. That decision, I believe, was one of the most important decisions that I have ever made. Young people who are at that particular time in their lives have the responsibility to make similar decisions. They have the important responsibility to choose whom to marry—not just whom to date.

Elder Bruce R. McConkie has said, "Nothing is more important than marrying the right person at the right time, in the right place, and by the right authority." We hope youth will avoid too quick courtships. It is important that each young person became acquainted with the person he plans to marry, that there is certainty that each is looking down the same pathway, with the same eternal objectives in mind.

Let us turn now to the third decision, *What will be my life's work.* I have counseled many returning missionaries who have asked this question. Frequently, we find that missionaries like to emulate their mission president. If he is an educator, a preponderant number of missionaries will want to be educators; if he is a businessman, a large number will want to study business; if he is a doctor, many of the missionaries will want to be physicians, for they naturally desire to emulate a man whom they respect and admire. My counsel to returning missionaries and to every youth is that they should study and prepare for their life's work in a field that they enjoy, because they are going to spend a good share of their lives in that field. I believe it should be a field that will challenge their intellect and a field that will make maximum utilization of their talents and their capabilities, and, finally, a field that will provide them sufficient remuneration to provide adequately for a companion and children. Such is a big order, but I bear testimony that these criteria are very important in choosing one's life's work.

I quote a passage of which President David O. McKay was fond: "You are the one who has to decide whether you'll do it or toss it aside; whether you'll strive for the goal that's afar, or just be content to stay where you are."

Adequate preparation enhances the ability to think and to decide. We find many people who are willing to alibi or who make excuse for a failure. During the early phases of World War II, a most vital decision was made by one of the great leaders of the Allied forces, Viscount Slim of Great Britain. Long after the war, he made this statement concerning this decision made in the battle for Khartoum in 1940: "Like so many generals whose plans have gone wrong, I could find plenty of excuses, but only one reason—myself! When two courses of action were open to me, I had not chosen, as a good commander should, the bolder. I had taken counsel of my fears."

I urge youth to not take counsel of their fears. I hope they will not say, "I'm not smart enough to study chemical engineering; hence, I'll study something less strenuous." "I can't apply myself sufficiently well to study this difficult subject or in this difficult field; hence, I'll choose the easier way." I plead with youth to choose the hard way and to tax their talents, and our Heavenly Father will make them equal to their tasks. If one should stumble, if one should take a course and get less than the A grade desired, I hope such a one will not let it discourage him. I hope that he will rise and try again.

Consider the experience of Admiral Chester W. Nimitz. When he graduated as an ensign in the U.S. Navy, he was given an old, decrepit destroyer as his first command. It was named the *Decatur*. It was all he could do to put the old destroyer in shape, and on one of its maiden voyages, Ensign Nimitz ran the ship aground. This resulted in a summary court-martial. Fortunately, he was found guilty only of neglect of duty, rather than a more serious offense. Had Chester Nimitz not been made of the stuff he was, that defeat could have ruined his career, but what did he do? He put that defeat behind him and went on to become the commanding admiral of the greatest sea force ever assembled in this world—the Pacific Fleet. He showed one and all that one defeat could not keep a good man down.

What will be my faith? Whom shall I marry? What will be my life's work? I am so grateful that we need not make those decisions without eternal help. Each one of us can have the guidance and direction of Heavenly Father if he strives for it. I would encourage us to learn and memorize the ninth section of the Doctrine and Covenants. This is a section that is frequently overlooked but that has a lesson for all of us. When we contemplate making a significant decision, may I suggest we go to our Heavenly Father in the manner in which the Prophet Joseph indicated the Lord advised him. The Lord said to the Prophet Joseph in that section: "Behold, you have not understood; you have supposed that I would give it unto you, when you took no thought save it was to ask me. But, behold, I say unto you, that you must study it out in your mind; then you must ask me if it be right, and if it is right I will cause that your bosom shall burn within you, therefore, you shall feel that it is right. But if it be not right you shall have no such feelings, but you shall have a stupor of thought that shall cause you to forget the thing which is wrong." (D&C 9:7-9.) Such is inspired direction for us in our day.

Recently I had the privilege of returning to Tahiti, to a people whom I dearly love. There I was talking to the mission president about the Tahitian people. They are known as some of the greatest seafaring people in all the world. The president, who spoke French but little English, was trying to describe to me the secret of the success of the Tahitian sea captains. He said, "They're amazing. The weather may be terrible; the vessels may be leaking; there may be no navigational aids except their inner feelings and the stars in the heavens, but they pray and they go!" And he repeated it three times: "They pray and they go; they pray and they go; they pray and they go!" There is a lesson for us in that statement. We need to pray and then we need to act; both are important.

In addition to the ninth section of the Doctrine and Covenants, in addition to the importance of prayer, I add a third dimension: Follow the prophets of God; and when we follow the prophets, we will be in safe territory. May I illustrate by sharing a most intimate experience from my own life.

I served in the United States Navy toward the end of World War II. I was what is called a seaman, the most elementary rank; then I qualified to be a seaman first class. Then I qualified to be a yeoman third class. The war ended, and I was discharged. I made a decision, however, that if ever I went back into the military, I wanted to be a commissioned officer. If one hasn't been in the military, he may not appreciate the difference between the apprentice seaman and the commissioned officer. You can best learn the difference by experience. Once learned, it's never forgotten. I thought, "No more mess kitchens for me. No more scrubbing of the decks if I can avoid it." Then I worked without respite to qualify for that commission. I joined the United States Naval Reserve; I attended drill every Monday night. I studied long hours, that I might qualify academically. I took every kind of examination you can imagine—mental, physical, emotional. Finally there came from Denver, Colorado, the welcome news: "You have been approved to receive the commission of an ensign in the United States Naval Reserve." I gleefully showed it to Sister Monson and said, "I made it! I made it!" She remarked enthusiastically, "You've worked hard to achieve it!"

But then circumstances changed. I was called to serve as a counselor in my ward bishopric. The bishop's council meeting was on the evening of my drill night. I knew there was an irreconcilable conflict. I didn't have the time to pursue the Naval Reserve and also my bishopric duties. What was I to do? A decision had to be made. Frankly, I prayed about it. I then went to see my former stake president, Elder Harold B. Lee. I sat across the table from him and mentioned to him how much I valued the Navy commission. He said to me, "Here's what you should do, Brother Monson. Write a letter to the Bureau of Naval Affairs and tell them that because of your call as a member of the bishopric, you can't accept the commission in the United States Naval Reserve." He continued, "Then write to the commandant of the Twelfth Naval District in San Francisco and tell him you'd like to be discharged from the reserve." I said, "Oh, Brother Lee, you don't understand the military. Of course they'll decline to give me that commission if I refuse, but the Twelfth Naval District isn't going to let any noncommissioned officer out of its hands with a war brewing in Korea. I could be stuck to go back in the service at a very low rating if I don't accept this commission. Are you sure this is the counsel you want me to receive?" He put his hand on my shoulder and in a fatherly way said, "Brother Monson, have more faith. The military is not for you."

I went to my home and placed a tear-stained commission back into its envelope with its accompanying letter and declined to accept it. I then wrote a letter to the Twelfth Naval District and requested a discharge from the Naval Reserve. My discharge from the Naval Reserve was in the last group processed before the outbreak of the Korean War. My headquarters unit was immediately activated. Just six weeks after being called as a counselor in a bishopric, I was called to be the bishop of my ward. I know my life would have been drastically different had I not followed the counsel of a prophet, had I not prayed about a decision, had I not come to appreciate an important truth: The wisdom of God ofttimes appears as foolishness to men, but the greatest single lesson we can learn in mortality is that when God speaks and a man obeys, that man will always be right.

May our Heavenly Father guide us and bless us in the decisions each of us will be called upon to make. If we want to see the light of heaven, if we desire to feel the inspiration of Almighty God, if we yearn to have that feeling within our bosom that our Heavenly Father is guiding us, let us "stand . . . in holy places, and be not moved." Then the Spirit of our Heavenly Father will be ours.

III

CALLED TO
THE WORK

20

*A*ccepting the Call to Serve

Some years ago I stood at a pulpit and noticed a little sign that only the speaker could see. The words on that sign were these: "Who stands at this pulpit, let him be humble." How I pray to my Heavenly Father that I might never forget the lesson I learned that day.

I feel to thank my Heavenly Father for His many blessings to me. I am grateful to have been born of goodly parents, whose parents were gathered out of the lands of Sweden and Scotland and England by humble missionaries who through the bearing of their testimonies touched the spirits of these wonderful people.

I am so grateful for my teachers and leaders in my boyhood and young manhood, in a humble, pioneer ward in a humble, pioneer stake. I am grateful for my sweet companion and for the influence for good that she has had upon my life, and to her dear mother, who had the courage in far-off Sweden to accept the gospel and to come to this country. I am so happy that the Lord has blessed us with three fine children, our youngest born to us in the mission field in Canada. I am grateful for these blessings.

I know that God lives, my brothers and sisters. There is no question in my mind. I know that this is His work, and I know that the sweetest experience in all this life is to feel His promptings as He directs us in the furtherance of His work. I have felt these promptings as a young bishop, guided to the homes where there was spiritual, or perhaps temporal, want. I felt it again in the mission field as I worked with your sons and your daughters—the missionaries of this great church who are a living witness and testimony to the world that this work is divine and that we are led by a prophet.

I think of a little sister, a French-Canadian sister, whose life was changed by the missionaries as her spirit was touched when she said goodbye to me and my wife in Quebec. She said, "President Monson, I may never see the prophet. I may never hear the prophet. But President, far better, now that I am a member of this church, I can obey the prophet."

My sincere prayer is that I might always obey our prophet and my brethren. I pledge my life, all that I may have. I will strive to the utmost of my ability to be what they would want me to be. I am grateful for the words of Jesus Christ, our Savior, when he said: "I stand at the door and knock: if any man hear my voice, and open the door, I will come in to him." (Revelation 3:20.)

I earnestly pray, my brothers and sisters, that my life might merit this promise from our Savior.*

---

*Acceptance message of Elder Thomas S. Monson given in Salt Lake Tabernacle on the occasion of his call to the apostleship, October 3, 1963.

21

*P*ersonal Promises

Some years ago I received an assignment to visit the stake conferences in Samoa and Australia. In Australia, that vast continent in the South Pacific, drouth is an ever-present problem. The Saints in the stakes and missions had written me through their leadership, asking that I join with them in a mighty prayer to our Heavenly Father that moisture would indeed accompany me on my projected visit.

En route to the conference appointments, I noted with some amusement the names of the stake presidents on whom I was to call. The first was President Percy Rivers; the second was William Waters. I called this to the attention of my traveling companion, only to be reminded by him that his name was Harry Brooks. We had a good laugh over this unusual assortment of names. Upon our arrival at the Sydney International Airport, we again were surprised to learn that the names of some awaiting us were Sister Rainey and Elder Hailstone. As I registered for my motel accommodation, the clerk could not locate the advance reservation. After some difficulty, he responded: "Oh, yes. Here it is. Mr. Thomas S. *Monsoon*." Moisture had become a common denominator.

You remember years ago in the elementary school arithmetic class the teacher would often speak of common denominators. I recognize today that there is a common denominator, common to you and to me, that binds us together as one. This common denominator is the individual call each one of us has received to fill an assignment in God's kingdom here upon the earth.

Have you ever been guilty of murmuring when an assignment came your way? Or have you accepted each calling with thanksgiving, knowing that our Heavenly Father will bless those whom he calls? I would hope that we would not lose the real vision of our cherished assignments; that we will not become swallowed up by the program alone. It is but a means to a goal. That objective, that eternal goal, is the same spoken of by the Lord and found in the Pearl of Great Price: "For behold, this is my work and my glory—to bring to pass the immortality and eternal life of man." (Moses 1:39.) Our duty in addition to saving ourselves is to guide others to the celestial kingdom of God.

May we ever remember that the mantle of leadership is not the cloak of comfort, but the robe of responsibility.

As we lead, let us be true shepherds. Most of us in the western part of the United States and Canada can, on occasion, see sheepherders driving their flocks to summer pasture or returning from the mountains as winter approaches. At times the sheepherder is slouched over the saddle, trailing his flock, with a host of anxious dogs yapping at the heels of the sheep and driving them onward in a determined course. How different is this scene from one that I viewed in Munich, Germany, where a true shepherd, with staff in hand, walked in front of his flock. The sheep recognized him as their leader, and indeed their shepherd, and followed him willingly wherever he would lead them.

When we, as leaders, set before others a proper example, they will follow us as sheep follow the true shepherd. Should our assignment be with youth, perhaps a few suggestions would assist us.

First, may we consider the problems we face. Second, may we listen to the pleas of youth. And third, may we promise to be leaders worthy of emulation. The problems facing youth today are more serious than in previous generations. All about us we see a lowering of moral standards. We see, accepted on every hand, the permissive society and all that goes with it. Fractured families likewise contribute to the problems we must meet and solve.

As we note the deterioration in moral standards, we think back to the great classic *The Decline and Fall of the Roman Empire*, by Edward Gibbon. He stated the reasons for the dissolution of the great political force that had held the civilized world together for more than five hundred years. The principal reasons included:

1. *Excessive spending by the central government.*

2. *Unwillingness of the young men to bear arms in defense of their country.*

3. *Overindulgence in luxury.*

4. *Widespread sexual immorality and easy divorce, which destroyed the integrity of family life.*

5. *Disregard for religion.*

That was Rome, fourteen hundred years ago. Does the picture seem to apply to us today? Just recently in one of the leading news magazines there appeared this letter to the editor: "There is no such thing as being immoral vs. being moral. If a person doesn't accept the established morals, he is simply living by his own standards: he is not being immoral."

This gives us a vision of what a rather substantial segment of the population really believes to be true, false though it most certainly is.

Oh that each youth in our charge came from a home presided over by the priesthood of God—a home in which there was family prayer and family home evening. Unfortunately, this is not the case. Some have little or no help from parents.

A young teenage girl, a member of the Church, wrote a touching letter to me. She said:

"Dear Brother Monson: I need counseling and advice *now*, and I need it from someone holding and honoring the priesthood who is in a position to have insight and give the right counsel.

"When I joined the Church I was engaged to a wonderful young man who had left for Vietnam three months before my baptism. He has since returned, and I spent Christmas vacation with him. Brother Monson, I broke the Word of Wisdom, was guilty of doubting the teachings of the Church, and slept with the boy I love several times. I don't in the least regret or feel ashamed of having shared my love with him, but I truly am ashamed of having taken a taste of rum and Coke. . . ."

This young lady really did need help. Her sense of values had been warped out of all proportion. Could she be representative of many others?

As we listen to the pleas of these young people, as we survey the problems that they encounter, we need more than an accurate diagnosis of the ailment. We require and search for a proper prescription for a lasting cure.

The pathway that will lead us to such a solution will require certain promises on our part as leaders. Will you, with me, commit yourself to the work of the Lord and consider the promises that would enhance your influence in the lives of youth? Let us consider such promises.

First, I promise to be willing. The Lord has declared: "The Lord requireth the heart and a willing mind; and the willing and obedient shall eat the good of the land of Zion in these last days." (D&C 64:34.)

Through such willing service, we will not be in the position of Shakespeare's Cardinal Wolsey, who, after a life of service to his king, stripped of his power, sadly lamented, "Had I but served my God with half the zeal I served my king, he would not in mine age have left me naked to mine enemies."

Second, I promise to be informed. Remember the counsel of the Lord: "Wherefore, now let every man learn his duty, and to act in the office in which he is appointed, in all diligence." (D&C 107:99.)

Third, I promise to be diligent. I will magnify my calling. What does it mean to magnify a calling? It means to build it up in dignity and importance, to make it honorable and commendable in the eyes of all mankind, to enlarge and strengthen it, to let the light of heaven shine through it to the view of other men. And how does one magnify a calling? Simply by performing the service that pertains to it. In short, we magnify our callings by learning what our duties are and then by performing them.

I pause when I think of the words of President John Taylor: "If you do not magnify your calling, God will hold you responsible for those whom you might have saved had you done your duty." Edgar A. Guest gave wise counsel in his poem "True Nobility":

Who does his task from day to day
And meets whatever comes his way,
Believing God has willed it so,
Has found true greatness here below.

Who guards his post, no matter where,
Believing God must need him there,
Although but lowly toil it be,
Has risen to nobility.

For great and low, there's but one test:
'Tis that each man shall do his best.
Who works with all the strength he can
Shall never die in debt to man.

Fourth, I promise to be prayerful. "Remember," said the Lord, "the worth of souls is great in the sight of God." (D&C 18:10.) As we develop an appreciation of this great truth, we will come to realize that we affect eternity; we determine destiny. We cannot succeed alone.

Our challenge is to eliminate the weakness of a youth standing alone and to substitute therefor the strength of youth and leaders serving together.

Fifth, I promise to be understanding. Among our youth are some who have transgressed the laws of God, who have been deceived by that evil one, and who seek from us an understanding heart and a guide to the pathway of repentance and exaltation in the kingdom of our Heavenly Father. We, in effect, stand at the crossroads of their lives.

Youth come in all varieties and sizes: short, tall, slim, and stout, lacking in confidence or filled with faith. My prayer is that we will indeed promise to be willing, informed, diligent, prayerful, and understanding; that we will aid each of them, so that together we may stay on that pathway which leads to exaltation in the kingdom of our Father, that as leaders or as teachers, when one day we are privileged to view the glory of our youth, we may say, "I'm glad I helped along the way."

22

*M*ore Blessed to Give
Than to Receive

As a boy I attended Sunday School in the Sixth-Seventh Ward of Pioneer and later of Temple View Stake. The ward population was rather transient, which resulted in an accelerated rate of turn-over with respect to the teachers in Sunday School. As boys and girls, we would just become acquainted with a particular teacher and grow to appreciate him when the Sunday School superintendent would visit the class and introduce a new teacher. Disappointment would fill each heart, and a breakdown of discipline would result.

Prospective teachers, hearing of the unsavory reputation of our particular class, would graciously decline to serve or suggest the possibility of teaching a different class where the students were more manageable. We took delight in our newly found status and determined to live up to the fears of the faculty.

One Sunday morning, a lovely young lady accompanied the superintendent into the classroom and was presented to us as a teacher who requested the opportunity to teach us. We learned that she had been a missionary and loved young people. Her name was Lucy Gertsch. She was beautiful, soft-spoken, and interested in us. She asked each class member to introduce himself and then she asked questions that gave her an understanding and insight into the background of each.

She told us of her girlhood in Midway, Utah, and as she described that beautiful valley she made its beauty live within us and we desired to visit the green fields she loved so much.

Those first few weeks were not easy. Boys don't become gentlemen overnight. Yet she never raised her voice. Somehow rudeness and boisterousness were incompatible with the beauty of her lessons. She made the scriptures actually live. We became personally acquainted with Samuel, David, Jacob, Nephi, and the Lord Jesus Christ. Our gospel scholarship grew. Our deportment improved. Our love for Lucy Gertsch knew no bounds.

We undertook a project to save nickels and dimes for what was to be a gigantic Christmas party. Sister Gertsch kept a careful record of our progress. As boys with typical appetites, we converted in our minds the monetary totals to cakes, cookies, pies, and ice cream. This was to be a glorious event. Never before had any of our teachers even suggested a social event like this was to be.

The summer months faded into autumn. Autumn turned to winter. Our party goal had been achieved. The class had grown. A good spirit prevailed.

None of us will forget that gray morning when our beloved teacher announced to us that the mother of one of our classmates had passed away. We thought of our own mothers and how much they meant to us. We felt sincere sorrow for Billy Devenport in his great loss.

The lesson that Sunday was from the book of Acts, chapter 20, verse 35: "Remember the words of the Lord Jesus, how he said, It is more blessed to give than to receive." At the conclusion of the presentation of a well-prepared lesson, Lucy Gertsch commented on the economic situation of Billy's family. These were depression times and money was scarce. With a twinkle in her eyes, she asked, "How would you like to follow this teaching of our Lord? How would you feel about taking our party fund, and, as a class, giving it to the Devenports as an expression of our love?" The decision was unanimous. We counted very carefully each penny and placed the total sum in a large envelope. A beautiful card was purchased and inscribed with our names.

This simple act of kindness welded us together as one. We learned through our own experience that it is indeed more blessed to give than to receive.

The years have flown. The old chapel is gone, a victim of industrialization. The boys and girls who learned, who laughed, who grew under the direction of that inspired teacher of truth, have never forgotten her love or her lessons.

Even today when we sing that old favorite:

Thanks for the Sabbath School. Hail to the day
When evil and error are fleeing away.
Thanks for our teachers who labor with care
That we in the light of the gospel may share—

—we think of Lucy Gertsch, our Sunday School teacher. For we loved Lucy and Lucy loved us.

23

Your Jericho Road

The word *road* is most intriguing. A generation ago movie moguls featured Bob Hope, Bing Crosby, and Dorothy Lamour in films entitled *The Road to Rio*, *The Road to Morocco*, and *The Road to Zanzibar*. Earlier yet, Rudyard Kipling immortalized another road when he penned the lines, "On the Road to Mandalay."

My thoughts have returned to a road made famous by the parable Jesus told. I speak of the road to Jericho. The Holy Bible enables us to relive the memorable event that made famous for all time the Jericho Road.

A certain lawyer stood and tempted the Master, saying, "What shall I do to inherit eternal life? He said unto him, What is written in the law? how readest thou? And he answering said, Thou shalt love the Lord thy God with all thy heart, and with all thy soul, and with all thy strength, and with all thy mind; and thy neighbour as thyself. And he said unto him, Thou hast answered right: this do, and thou shalt live.

"But he, willing to justify himself, said unto Jesus, And who is my neighbour? And Jesus answering said, A certain man went down from Jerusalem to Jericho, and fell among thieves, which stripped him of his raiment, and wounded him, and departed, leaving him half dead.

"And by chance there came down a certain priest that

way: and when he saw him, he passed by on the other side. And likewise a Levite, when he was at the place, came and looked on him, and passed by on the other side.

"But a certain Samaritan, as he journeyed, came where he was: and when he saw him, he had compassion on him, And went to him, and bound up his wounds, pouring in oil and wine, and set him on his own beast, and brought him to an inn, and took care of him. And on the morrow when he departed, he took out two pence, and gave them to the host, and said unto him, Take care of him; and whatsoever thou spendest more, when I come again, I will repay thee.

"Which now of these three, thinkest thou, was neighbour unto him that fell among the thieves? And he said, He that shewed mercy on him. Then said Jesus unto him, Go, and do thou likewise." (Luke 10:25-37.)

Each of us, in the journey through mortality, will travel his own Jericho Road. What will be your experience? What will be mine? Will I fail to notice him who has fallen among thieves and requires my help? Will you? Will I be one who sees the injured and hears his plea, yet crosses to the other side? Will you? Or will I be one who sees, who hears, who pauses, and who helps? Will you?

Jesus provided our watchword, "Go, and do thou likewise." When we obey that declaration, there opens to our view a vista of joy seldom equaled and never surpassed.

Now the Jericho Road may not be clearly marked. Neither may the injured cry out, that we may hear. But when we walk in the steps of that good Samaritan, we walk the pathway that leads to perfection.

Note the many examples provided by the Master: the crippled man at the pool of Bethesda; the woman taken in adultery; the woman at Jacob's well; the daughter of Jairus; Lazarus, brother of Mary and Martha—each represented a casualty on the Jericho Road. Each needed help.

To the cripple at Bethesda, Jesus said: "Rise, take up thy bed, and walk." (John 5:8.) To the sinful woman came the counsel, "Go, and sin no more." (John 8:11.) To her who came to draw water, He provided a well of water springing up into everlasting life. (John 4:14.) To the dead daughter of Jairus came the command, "Damsel, I say unto thee, arise." (Mark 5:41.) To the entombed Lazarus the memorable words, "Lazarus, come forth." (John 11:43.)

One may well ask the penetrating question: These accounts pertained to the Redeemer of the world. Can there actually occur in my own life, on my Jericho Road, such a treasured experience?

My answer is a resounding yes. Let me share with you two such examples—first, the account of one who was injured and was helped; and second, the learning experience of one who traveled the Jericho Road.

Some years ago there went to his eternal reward one of the kindest and most loved men to grace the earth. I speak of Louis C. Jacobsen. He ministered to those in need, he helped the immigrant to find employment, and he delivered more sermons at more funeral services than any other person I have known.

One day while in a reflective mood, Louis Jacobsen told me of his boyhood. He was the son of a poor Danish widow. He was small in stature, not comely in appearance—easily the object of his classmates' thoughtless jokes. In Sunday School one Sabbath morning, the children made light of his patched trousers and his worn shirt. Too proud to cry, tiny Louis fled from the chapel, stopping at last, out of breath, to sit and rest on the curb that ran along Third West Street in Salt Lake City. Clear water flowed along the gutter next to the curb where Louis sat. From his pocket he took a piece of paper that contained the outlined Sunday School lesson and skillfully shaped a paper boat, which he launched on the flowing water. From his hurt boyish heart came the determined words, "I'll never go back."

Suddenly, through his tears Louis saw reflected in the water the image of a large and well-dressed man. Louis turned his face upward and recognized George Burbidge, the Sunday School superintendent. "May I sit down with you?" asked the kind leader. Louis nodded affirmatively. There on the gutter's curb sat a good Samaritan ministering to one who surely was in need. Several boats were formed and launched while the conversation continued. At last the leader stood and, with a boy's hand tightly clutching his, they returned to Sunday School. Later Louis himself presided over that same Sunday School. Throughout his long life of service, he never failed to acknowledge the traveler who rescued him along a Jericho Road.

When I first learned of that far-reaching experience, I reflected on the words:

He stood at the crossroads all alone,
The sunlight in his face.
He had no thought for the world unknown—
He was set for a manly race.
But the roads stretched east and the roads stretched west,
And the lad knew not which road was best.
So he chose the road that led him down,
And he lost the race and the victor's crown.
He was caught at last in an angry snare
Because no one stood at the crossroads there
To show him the better road.

Another day at the self-same place
A boy with high hopes stood.
He, too, was set for a manly race;
He, too, was seeking the things that were good.
But one was there whom the roads did know,

And that one showed him which way to go.
So he turned from the road that would lead him down,
And he won the race and the victor's crown.
He walks today the highway fair
Because one stood at the crossroads there
To show him the better way.

May I relate to you my first journey along a personal Jericho Road. In about my tenth year, as Christmas approached, I yearned as only a boy can yearn for an electric train. My desire was not to receive the economical and everywhere-to-be-found wind-up model train; rather, I wanted one that operated through the miracle of electricity. The times were those of economic depression, yet Mother and Dad, through some sacrifice, I am sure, presented to me on Christmas morning a beautiful electric train.

For hours I operated the transformer, watching the engine first pull its cars forward, then push them backward around the track. Mother entered the living room and said to me that she had purchased a wind-up train for Mrs. Hansen's son Mark, who lived down the lane. I asked if I could see the train. The engine was short and blocky—not long and sleek like the expensive model I had received. However, I did take notice of an oil tanker car that was part of his inexpensive set. My train had no such car, and pangs of envy began to be felt. I put up such a fuss that Mother succumbed to my pleadings and handed me the oil tanker car. She said, "If you need it more than Mark, you take it." I put it with my train set and felt pleased with the result.

Mother and I took the remaining cars and the engine down to Mark Hansen. The young boy was a year or two older than I. He had never anticipated such a gift and was thrilled beyond words. He wound the key in his engine, it not being electric like mine, and was overjoyed as the engine and two cars, plus a caboose, went around the track. Mother wisely

157

asked, "What do you think of Mark's train, Tommy?" I felt a keen sense of guilt and became very much aware of my selfishness. I said to Mother, "Wait just a moment—I'll be right back."

As swiftly as my legs could carry me, I ran to our home, picked up the oil tanker car, plus an additional car of my own, ran back down the lane to the Hansen home, and said joyfully to Mark, "We forgot to bring two cars that belong to your train." Mark coupled the two extra cars to his set. I watched the engine make its labored way around the track and felt a supreme joy difficult to describe and impossible to forget.

Mother and I left the Hansen home and slowly walked up the street. She, who, with her hand in God's, had entered into the valley of the shadow of death to bring me, her son, across the bridge of life, now took me by the hand; and together we returned homeward by way of our private Jericho Road.

Some remember mother for her rhymes recited, others for her music played, songs sung, favors bestowed, or stories told; but I remember best that day we together traveled our Jericho Road and, like the good Samaritan, found a cherished opportunity to help.

My brothers and sisters, today there are hearts to gladden, there are deeds to be done—even precious souls to save. The sick, the weary, the hungry, the cold, the injured, the lonely, the aged, the wanderer, all cry out for our help.

The road signs of life enticingly invite every traveler: this way to fame; this way to affluence; this way to popularity; this way to luxury. May we pause at the crossroads before we continue our journey. May we listen for that still, small voice which ever so gently beckons, "Come, follow me. This way to Jericho." Then may each of us follow Him along that Jericho Road which leads to life eternal.

24

*B*orn of Goodly Parents

As we open the Book of Mormon, we read the salutation, "I, Nephi, having been born of goodly parents. . . ." What a beautiful message! What an example for you and me if we will but say the same: "I, Tom; I, Jane; I, Scott, having been born of goodly parents." How will we finish that phrase? Nephi went and did what the Lord commanded him to do. What will we do? What will be our plan? What will be our purpose as we respond to that introduction, "I, having been born of goodly parents. . . ."

May I offer three suggestions for our consideration:

1. *Find faith;*
2. *Learn love;*
3. *Choose Christ.*

How does one find faith? We do not find it by reading about it in a book; we must discover faith for ourselves. President David O. McKay taught: "The greatest battle of life is fought within the silent chambers of your own soul." It is a good thing for us to sit down and commune with ourselves, to come to an understanding of ourselves and decide in that silent moment what our duty is to family, to church, to country, and to our fellowmen.

Little children sometimes provide interesting examples of faith and devotion. I remember that when our family was very small, Sister Monson and I were praying for a particular sister in our ward who was afflicted with cancer. Her name was Margaret Lister. Each night we would kneel by the side of our bed and pray for Sister Lister. On one occasion we invited our little six-year-old boy to offer the prayer. He became a little confused in his child mind and in the prayer said, "Heavenly Father, bless Mother, Father, and Sister Lister, Henny Penny, Turkey Lurkey, and Chicken Licken and all the rest of the animals." It was all that Sister Monson and I could do to remain serious. A strange thing happened. Sister Lister had a remarkable recovery. I'm simple enough to think that her recovery may well have been assisted by the pleading of a first grade student venturing to call upon his Heavenly Father in prayer.

Some time ago, I jotted down from one of our national magazines comments interesting to me that children had prepared. They were entitled "What Children Think of God."

One wrote, "Dear God, I wished on a star two times but nothing happened. Now what? Ann." I suppose some of us do that.

Another one said, "Dear God, If you made the rule for kids to take out the garbage, please change it."

Another voice, "Dear Holy God, Would you make it so that there wouldn't be any more wars and so everyone could vote. Also everybody should have a lot of fun. Nancy."

Another one: "Dear God, Charles my cat got run over and if you made it happen, you have to tell me why. Harvey."

I enjoyed this one: "Dear God, I read your book and I like it." Then he says, "I would like to write a book someday with the same kind of stories. God, where do you get your ideas? Best wishes, Mark."

Where did God get His ideas? Whence came His stories?

He didn't read about them; He experienced them, and that's how we find faith. To discover faith, we must experience it.

Let me share with you an item very close to my heart. A friend whom I had known a long while, a robust athlete, an all-star football player, was stricken with a malady that left him paralyzed. His name was Stan Cockrell. The doctors said he would never walk again. I was as crestfallen as was he. Then one day I was swimming at the Deseret Gymnasium. As I powered myself across the pool, suddenly my mind dwelt upon my friend Stan, then a patient at the University Hospital in Salt Lake City, unable to swim, unable to walk. The longer I swam, the more I had the impression and the direction that he needed me. Quickly I left the pool, dressed, and went immediately to the University Hospital. There I found my friend in the depths of despair, ready to abandon everything he held precious. I told him how I happened to be there. I said, "I didn't just come, Stan. The Lord knew you needed a blessing, and He knew that you needed it from one who knew you. He took occasion to impress this upon me while I was swimming with the full use of my body, knowing that you were handicapped with a limited use of your body." A blessing was provided.

The Spirit of the Lord was with us. Day by day, Stan Cockrell grew stronger.

A year later there was a knock at my office door, and in walked my friend Stan, aided by a cane. Here was one of whom it had been said he would never walk again. Then he handed the cane to his son, who was to be set apart for a mission, and walked over to my desk. What a joy! What a moment of thanksgiving! We set his son apart as a missionary to go to the Scotland Glasgow Mission. Then, just a few months ago in the holy temple, witnessing the marriage of his daughter, was my friend Stan Cockrell, standing there without a crutch, without a walker, without a cane. In one sentence he described the feelings of his heart. "Tom," he said, "I never doubted." Think of it: "I never doubted."

President Stephen L Richards taught, "Faith and doubt cannot exist in the same mind at the same time, for one will dispel the other." My plea is that we will find faith by experiencing faith in action. The opportunity is ours. Let us grasp it and retain it.

Now to the second point: learn love. How are we going to learn love? I would hope that most of us have already learned love as it comes from our mothers and fathers. My grandfather was a quiet Scotsman. I learned many lessons from him. As a boy I would frequently seek a nickel from him for an ice cream. We used to call it a Milk Nickel, and that's all it cost. Grandpa would counsel me on the virtue of thrift. On one occasion I bought a dog, a German short-haired pointer. I was so proud of that dog. I paid twenty-five dollars for him, and that was a fortune to me. I was attempting to train the young dog with a leash, teaching him to "heel" as I walked down the street. I made the mistake of walking in front of my grandfather's home, and he saw what I was doing. He called me over, took a look at the dog, then said, "Tom, how much did you give for that dog?" I didn't have the heart to tell him the truth. I gingerly said, "Five dollars." He responded, "You dern fool! You got bit. You paid four dollars and seventy-five cents too much!" I looked at the poor hound and I realized that I had indeed paid too much.

That wasn't the only lesson I learned from Grandpa, nor was receiving the generous offer of a nickel for an ice cream the lesson I best remember. The lesson for which I best remember my grandfather was a lesson wherein he taught me the principle of love. An elderly man from England lived on our street. We called him "Old Bob," but his name was Robert Dick. A widower and impoverished, he lived alone in a small old adobe house. Word came to him that the home was going to be demolished. This was devastating to him. He had nowhere to go; no family to whom he might turn. He walked across the street, sat on the old porch swing with my grandfather, and told him his lament. Then he said to my grandfather, "Mr. Condie, you have an old house next door to your home, and that old house is not occupied. It will take most of what I have, but could I please rent a part of that home?" I was sitting on the swing. I think I was not more than eight or nine years of age, but I was listening as children do. I remember my grandfather taking "Old Bob" by the hand and saying, "Mr. Dick, you move your things into that house of mine next door, and it won't cost you a cent. You can stay there as long as you like. And remember, nobody is ever going to put you out." I was so proud of my grandfather and his generosity as I learned from that conversation a lesson of love.

"Old Bob" lived in that house until the day that he died. Every Sunday afternoon as Mother would serve the Sunday dinner, before we sat down to the table she would prepare a plate, put some wax paper over it, hand it to me, and say, "Take this food down to 'Old Bob' and then hurry back for dinner." I'd hurry down the street to that old house, walk into the darkened living room where the kerosene lantern stood, and hand "Old Bob" the filled plate. He would smile and attempt to offer me a dime, but my mother had told me, "If he offers you money, tell him 'Thank you, the dinner isn't for sale.'" Then he would hand me the plate I had brought the previous Sunday, all washed and polished, and would put his arm around me and say, "Tell your mother 'Thank you.'" As I would hurry back up the street, hungry as a boy can be, I'd run into the house and say to Mother, "'Old Bob' says 'Thank you.'" I didn't know then why Mother's eyes would glisten, and why she would be unusually quiet when I brought to her that message, but I know now—because Mother had learned love. And I, through that experience, learned love.

Point three: choose Christ. Battles are not won in a day. Sometimes they are won only in a lifetime of service and activity.

I recall an officer of the seminary at Olympus High School in Salt Lake City—a young boy by the name of Edward Engh. He was handicapped and was confined to a wheelchair. When our daughter, who was a seminary officer, brought the officers to our home, Ed was present. We had a delightful time with the group that evening. Then this boy, in such a difficult situation, turned to me and said, "Brother Monson, you're on the Church Missionary Committee, aren't you?" I said I was. He said, "Brother Monson, all my life I've wanted to be a missionary. May I have that opportunity?" And as I looked at him, I saw no way. I comforted him in private and said, "Ed, you can be a missionary here at home, but I think it would be difficult for you to be a missionary anywhere else." Then I said, "Have you thought of a stake mission? Would you consider that?"

He was called on a stake mission and gave a fine account of himself. But he wanted to be a full-time missionary; he wanted to serve as other young men did, to have a farewell, to get a new set of scriptures, to go to the Missionary Training Center, and then to arrive in a field of labor. Finally, after about four long years, his day of glory came; and through the kindness of a particular mission president who knew him, and through the kindness of a missionary staff who wanted him, and through the faith of a mother and a father who loved him, and through the courage of a boy who honored father and honored mother and who honored the Lord, Edward Engh received his missionary call to the Canada Vancouver Mission. I'd like to share with you a letter that his mission president wrote to me:

"Dear Elder Monson, I felt impressed to write you regarding the progress of this great elder. Elder Engh has already become a legend in the mission. He has established a standard of faith and dedication in the short time he has been here. He is serving in the mission office as the recorder. He passed off his discussions in record time, and he and his companion have already baptized and lead their district in teaching. The mission work seems to agree with him. He's in good health. We're watching him carefully as to rest and diet, but he has not required any extra attention. He has a great and loving companion. These two elders truly have a Christlike love for one another, which was demonstrated when Elder Engh first arrived and expressed some concern for one of the themes of the mission, 'Lengthen Your Stride.' Elder Engh said to his companion, 'How can I lengthen my stride? I can't even walk!' His companion responded, 'That's okay, Elder Engh, we'll just have to get you some bigger wheels.'

"Elder Engh is a great inspiration to all of us. In a recent conference he told the other missionaries, 'I don't dare complain about my condition, my surroundings, my companion, the rain, or anything else. You see, I prayed night and day to be called on a mission, and the Lord answered my prayer. And now I'm here and I would not do anything to disappoint the Lord.' "

May I suggest how we can find faith, learn love, and choose Christ? When we recognize sin, shun it. When we make a mistake, admit it. When we receive a gift, share it. When we enjoy freedom, protect it. When we have the truth, live it. When we have a duty, do it. Then eternal glory will be ours.

It was Napoleon who said of his troops, "I have always found you on the road to glory." I pray that our Heavenly Father may always find you and me not only on the road to glory, but on the road to eternal life, even the highest degree of glory in the celestial kingdom of our Father.

165

25

*F*ormula for Success

During the meridian of time the apostle Peter declared: "Ye are a chosen generation, a royal priesthood, an holy nation, a peculiar people; that ye should shew forth the praises of him who hath called you out of darkness into his marvellous light." (1 Peter 2:9.) This is the destiny of every Latter-day Saint if he or she will live for the fulfillment of that destiny.

When the Savior was upon the earth, He taught with the use of parables. Remember the parable of the wise and the foolish virgins who were instructed to fill their precious lamps with oil, and you will recall that five prepared properly and five did not prepare. Then came the day when the bridegroom appeared, and there was not additional oil to fill the lamps of those who were unprepared. Do you recall the rebuke of the Master on that occasion? "Verily I say unto you, I know you not." (Matthew 25:12.) A great lesson in preparation.

We recall also the parable of the talents. One was given five talents, another four, three, two, and so on. How pleased was the master with those individuals who had multiplied their talents and had put them to good use. How unhappy he was with the person who had but one talent and who, out of fear of losing that one talent, buried it in the ground. We know his words: "Cast ye the unprofitable servant into outer darkness." (Matthew 25:30.)

And we remember the parable of the fig tree. The fig tree had leaves, but produced no fruit; and the tree was commanded never to produce again. Remember the particular rebuke: "Let no fruit grow on thee henceforward for ever." Then came the response of those who observed the fulfillment of this command: "How soon is the fig tree withered away!" (Matthew 21:19-20.)

From those parables I would like to suggest that if we are really to be a chosen generation, a royal priesthood, we have the responsibility to be prepared, to be productive, to be faithful, and to be fruitful as well. What we need, as we journey along through this period known as mortality, is a compass to chart our course, a map to guide our footsteps, and a pattern whereby we might mold and shape our very lives. May I share with you a formula that in my judgment will help you and help me to journey well through mortality and to that great reward of exaltation in the celestial kingdom of our Heavenly Father.

First, fill your mind with truth; second, fill your life with service; and third, fill your heart with love.

Let's talk about each one of the parts of the formula and see if each does not find lodgment within the human heart. First, fill your mind with truth. I'd like to suggest that when we search for truth, we search among those books and in those places where truth is most likely to be found. I've often referred to a simple couplet: "You do not find truth groveling through error. You find truth by searching the holy word of God." There are those who for direction and inspiration turn to the philosophies of man. There a smattering of truth may be found, but not the entire spectrum. Sometimes the truth of such philosophies is based upon a shallow foundation. I think of the story of the monkey who was in a cage situated on the flight pattern near a large airport. The monkey became terrified initially as a plane would fly overhead, and in his fright he would rattle the bars of his cage. Soon he realized that as he rattled the bars of his cage, the airplane would fly away, and he would be safe. The monkey no doubt felt that the rattling of the bars of the cage caused the airplane, out of fright of him, to pass beyond and leave him alone. Of course the rattling of the bars of the cage had nothing to do with the departure of the airplane, and so it is with some of man's philosophies. We need to turn to the truth of God.

I like the words of Louisa May Alcott, author of that all-time classic *Little Women*, who wrote:

> *I do not ask for any crown*
> *But that which all may win;*
> *Nor try to conquer any world*
> *Except the one within.*

You and I have the responsibility to learn the word of God, to understand the word of God, and then to live His word. By so doing, we will find that we have learned and accepted the truth. The Prophet Joseph Smith provided direct counsel. He said simply, "When I find out what God wants me to do, I do it!"

David M. Kennedy, special representative of the First Presidency, made a significant statement when he was called to be the Secretary of the Treasury of the United States. In an interview with the press, he was asked by a reporter if he believed in prayer. He boldly answered, "I believe in prayer, and I pray," teaching the entire world that truth can come when one seeks help from his Heavenly Father.

This is a day when time is precious. This is a time when we cannot afford not to be engaged in an earnest search for truth. May we fill our minds with truth.

The second part of the formula is: Fill your life with service. From the Book of Mormon we learn, "When ye are in the service of your fellow beings ye are only in the service of your

God." (Mosiah 2:17.) Missionaries particularly have a wonderful opportunity to give of their full time in sharing with all the world that commodity of such priceless value—a testimony of the gospel. To missionaries I declare that you have been called of God by prophecy and are divinely commissioned and sent forth in your sacred calling.

For a number of years it was my opportunity to serve as a member of the Missionary Executive Committee and to profit from the leadership of President Spencer W. Kimball, who was chairman of the committee. On one occasion I remember having read the detail on a particular missionary candidate, and President Kimball indicated that the young man would go, I believe, to London, England. Then he said, "No. That is not correct. Send the young man to the Denmark Copenhagen Mission." I looked on the form and noticed that I had overlooked reading a very important statement from the stake president. I said, "President Kimball, have you ever seen this particular form before?" "No," he replied. "Look at what the stake president has written," I continued. " 'The grandfather of this missionary candidate is an immigrant from the land of Denmark. He is our stake patriarch. The missionary candidate was promised in his patriarchal blessing that if he lived true and faithful he would return to the land of his forebears, that he might preach the gospel in that particular land.' " President Kimball nodded his approval and said, "The Lord's will has been made known today."

Missionaries should go forward knowing that they are in the service of God, that they are going to share that most precious commodity—their testimonies. Remember, a testimony is perishable. That which you selfishly keep, you lose; that which you willingly share, you keep. All of us benefit when we remember to magnify our callings.

Many of us remember a beloved General Authority, now deceased, even William J. Critchlow. I was particularly fond of

Brother Critchlow. I had the opportunity of accompanying him and Sister Critchlow to a number of stake conferences when I served on several priesthood committees. Brother Critchlow related to a conference a simple story that taught me a never-to-be forgotten lesson about doing one's duty, about rendering service to one's fellowmen. It was a fairy tale, yet it had the ring of profound truth.

The story was about a young man named Rupert, who lived in the high mountain country. His vocation was very humble: he cared for the sheep and the goats that belonged to the tiny flock his grandmother kept. Rupert's mother and father were dead. Every morning Rupert would take the sheep and the goats to the mountain pastures, watch them throughout the day, and perhaps midway through the day take them to the little brook where they would obtain sufficient water; then in the evening he would bring them home. One day a courier went through all the little villages, including the one where Rupert lived, and posted a bulletin upon a large tree in each village—a bulletin that indicated that the precious emerald of the king of the land had been lost. The king had been out riding and the emerald had torn away from the chain that held it about his neck and had been lost. A fabulous reward was offered to whoever could retrieve the king's emerald.

Rupert said to his grandmother, "I'm going to go search for the king's emerald, because I know if I could find it and should obtain the reward, you could live with more comfort than we are able to provide through the small flock of sheep and goats that I tend." His grandmother said to him, "No, Rupert. If you should go on a search for the king's emerald, who would tend the sheep and who would tend the goats?" And then she counseled him to go about his daily work.

Rupert followed his grandmother's advice. He took the sheep and the goats to the mountain pasture, as he had done every day. Then, as the day warmed, he brought them down to a friendly brook. There, as boys are wont to do, he lay prone on his stomach, that he might drink his fill of the clear, cool waters. As he did so, he noticed something sparkling within the brook. He thought for a moment, "Could it possibly be?" and plunged his hand into the stream, bringing forth the king's emerald. Clutching it tightly, he ran all the way home to his grandmother and said, "Grandmother, I have found the king's emerald! I have found the king's emerald!" He then explained to her, "Perhaps as the king's horse jumped the brook the emerald fell from the chain that held it about the king's neck, but I have it now within my hands, and the reward shall be yours." His grandmother took him aside and said, "Remember, my boy, you would never have found the king's emerald had you not been performing your duty."

Do your duty; that is best. Leave unto the Lord the rest.

Our third part of the formula is: Fill your heart with love. I remember watching on television a very exciting baseball game between evenly matched teams. One of the teams had one of the greatest home run hitters of all time. After the game a reporter interviewed him. He didn't talk too much about home runs or runs batted in. He talked about his father. The ball player was Hank Aaron. He did not have very much of this world's goods when he was a young boy, but he loved baseball. It consumed his life. He said that he and his father used to sit in an old, abandoned car that was in the rear of their lot and talk for hour after hour. One day Hank said to his dad, "I'm going to quit school, Dad. I'm going to go to work so I can play baseball." And Herbert Aaron said to his son, "My boy, I quit school because I had to, but you're not going to quit school. Every morning of your young life I've put fifty cents on the table, that you might buy your lunch that day. And I take twenty-five cents with me, that I might buy my lunch. Your education means more to me than my lunch. I want you to

172

have what I never had." Hank Aaron said that every time he thought about that fifty-cent piece that his father put on the table every day, he thought how much that fifty cents meant to his father. It conveyed to him how much his schooling meant to his father. Hank Aaron said, "I never had too much difficulty staying in school when I reflected upon the love my father had for me. As a result of reflecting upon the love of my father, I obtained my schooling and played a lot of baseball." That was putting it mildly from the greatest home run threat that ever stepped up to a baseball diamond—Henry Aaron.

Let us turn from Hank Aaron to a United Press International news release I read a short time ago from Los Angeles: "A blind father rescued his tiny daughter from drowning in the new swimming pool that had been installed in the neighborhood." Then the story went on to describe just how this had been accomplished. The blind father had heard a splash when his little girl, who could not swim, fell into the pool. He was frantic and wondered how he might help her. It was evening, and she was the only one in the pool. He got upon his hands and knees and crawled around the side of the pool and listened for the air bubbles that came from that little girl, as she was actually in the process of drowning. Then, with a heightened sense of hearing, he followed carefully the sound of those air bubbles and, in one desperate attempt, with love in his heart and a prayer within his soul, he jumped into the pool and grasped his precious daughter and brought her to the side and to safety. Love prompts such miracles.

When I think of love, I think of Abraham Lincoln, one of the great presidents of the United States. He was also one of our greatest writers and orators. I think that I have never read words that better describe the love that a man can have for others than the love he described as he penned a letter to a mother who had lost all her sons in the Civil War. It is known as the Lydia Bixby Letter. Note carefully the words of Abraham Lincoln and see if you don't feel within your heart the love that filled his:

"Dear Madam:

"I have just been shown, in the files of the War Department, a statement of the Adjutant General of Massachusetts that you are the mother of five sons who died gloriously on the field of battle.

"I feel how weak and fruitless must be any words of mine which should attempt to beguile you from the grief of a loss so overwhelming, but I cannot refrain from tendering to you the consolation that may be found in the thanks of the republic they died to save.

"I pray that our Heavenly Father may assuage the anguish of your bereavement and leave you only the cherished memory of the loved and lost and the solemn pride that must be yours to have laid so costly a sacrifice upon the altar of freedom.

Yours very sincerely and respectfully,
A. Lincoln"

In our sacrament meetings we frequently sing the hymn . . .

I stand all amazed at the love Jesus offers me;
Confused at the grace that so fully he proffers me;
I tremble to know that for me he was crucified,
That for me a sinner, he suffered, he bled and died.

I think of his hands pierced and bleeding to pay the debt!
Such mercy, such love, and devotion can I forget?
No, no, I will praise and adore at the mercy seat,
Until at the glorified throne I kneel at his feet.

HYMNS, NO. 80

I stand all amazed at the love Jesus offers me and the love Jesus offers you. I think of the love He provided in Gethsemane. I think of the love He provided in the wilderness. I think of the love He provided at the tomb of Lazarus; of the love He demonstrated on Golgotha's Hill, at the open tomb, and, yes, when He appeared in that Sacred Grove with His Father and spoke those memorable words to Joseph Smith. I thank God for His love in sharing His Only Begotten Son in the flesh, even Jesus Christ, for you and me. I thank the Lord for the love He demonstrated by providing His life, that we might have life eternal.

Jesus is more than a teacher. Jesus is the Savior of the world. He is the Redeemer of all mankind. He is the Son of God. He showed the way. You may recall that Jesus filled His mind with truth, and Jesus filled His life with service, and Jesus filled His heart with love. When we follow that example, we shall never hear those words of rebuke that came from the parables. We shall never find that we have empty lamps. We shall never discover that our homes have been left unto us desolate. We shall never determine that we have been found unfruitful in the kingdom of God. Rather, when you and I follow carefully the parts of this formula and literally fill our minds with truth, fill our lives with service, and fill our hearts with love, we may qualify to hear one day that statement of our Savior, "Well done, thou good and faithful servant: thou hast been faithful over a few things, I will make thee ruler over many things: enter thou into the joy of thy lord." (Matthew 25:21.)

My prayer is that we may so conduct ourselves that we may merit that plaudit from our Lord and Savior. I pray that each one of us may so live that he may qualify for the blessing of the Lord when He declared: "I, the Lord, am merciful and gracious unto those who fear me, and delight to honor those who serve me in righteousness and in truth unto the end. Great shall be their reward and eternal shall be their glory." (D&C 76:5-6.)

26

*T*he Lord's Way

Salt Lake City is a mecca for tourists from all parts of the globe. Thousands throng to the beautiful ski slopes of Alta, Brighton, Park City, and Snowbird each winter. Each summer the canyons of Bryce and Zion National Parks host thousands more. An attraction for all seasons is Temple Square, with its historic tabernacle, lofty, spired temple, and the beautiful visitors center, which bids to one and all a friendly welcome.

Situated somewhat off the beaten path, away from the crowd, is yet another famous square. Here in a quiet fashion, motivated by a Christlike love, elderly and handicapped workers serve one another after the divine plan of the Master. I speak of Welfare Square, sometimes known as the Bishop's Storehouse. At this central location and at numerous other sites throughout the world, fruits and vegetables are canned and commodities are processed, labeled, stored, and distributed to those persons who are in need. There is no sign of government dole nor the exchange of currency here, since only the signed order from an ordained bishop is honored.

Journalists marvel at this unique welfare plan and write glowingly of a people who take justifiable pride in the independence of caring for their own. Most frequently the curious and pleasantly surprised visitor asks three fundamental questions: (1) How does this plan operate? (2) How is it financed?

(3) What prompts such devotion on the part of every worker?

Over the years it has been my pleasant opportunity to supply many with the answers to these sincerely asked questions. To the question "How does this plan operate?" I usually respond by mentioning that I had the privilege during the period 1950 through 1955 to preside as a bishop over one thousand members of the Church, situated in the central part of Salt Lake City. In the congregation were eighty-six widows and perhaps forty families who were judged to be in need, at varying times and to some extent, of welfare assistance. Each year I, along with the thousands of other bishops, would prepare a commodity requirement budget estimating the needs of our people for the coming year. All such budgets were carefully reviewed and compiled and specific assignments given to units of the Church, that the requirements of the needy might be met.

In one ecclesiastical unit the Church members would produce beef, in another oranges, in another vegetables or wheat—even a variety of staples, that the storehouses might be filled and the elderly and needy supplied. The Lord provided the way when he declared, "And the storehouse shall be kept by the consecrations of the church; and the widows and orphans shall be provided for, as also the poor." (D&C 83:6.) Then the reminder, "But it must needs be done in mine own way." (D&C 104:16.)

In the vicinity where I lived and served, we operated a poultry project. Most of the time it was an efficiently operated project supplying to the storehouse thousands of dozens of fresh eggs and hundreds of pounds of dressed poultry. On a few occasions, however, the experience of being volunteer city farmers provided not only blisters on the hands, but also frustration of heart and mind. For instance, I shall ever remember the time we gathered the teenage Aaronic Priesthood young men to really give the poultry project a spring cleaning treatment. Our enthusiastic and energetic throng gathered at the project and, in a speedy fashion, uprooted, gathered, and burned large quantities of weeds and debris. By the light of the glowing bonfires we ate hot dogs and congratulated ourselves on a job well done. The project was now neat and tidy. However, there was just one disastrous problem. The noise and the fires had so disturbed the fragile and temperamental population of five thousand laying hens that most of them went into a sudden moult and ceased laying. Thereafter we tolerated a few weeds, that we might produce more eggs.

No member of The Church of Jesus Christ of Latter-day Saints who has canned peas, topped beets, hauled hay, or shoveled coal in such a cause ever forgets or regrets the experience of helping provide for those in need. Devoted men and women help to operate this vast and inspired program. In reality, the plan would never succeed on effort alone, for this program operates through faith after the way of the Lord.

In response to the second question, "How is your welfare plan financed?" one needs but to describe the fast offering principle. The prophet Isaiah described the true fast by asking, "Is it not to deal thy bread to the hungry, and that thou bring the poor that are cast out to thy house? when thou seest the naked, that thou cover him; and that thou hide not thyself from thine own flesh?

"Then shall the light break forth as the morning, and thine health shall spring forth speedily: and thy righteousness shall go before thee; the glory of the Lord shall be thy reward.

"Then shalt thou call, and the Lord shall answer; thou shalt cry, and he shall say, Here I am. . . .

"And the Lord shall guide thee continually, and satisfy thy soul in drought, . . . and thou shalt be like a watered garden, and like a spring of water, whose waters fail not." (Isaiah 58:7-9, 11.)

Guided by this principle, in a plan outlined and taught by

inspired prophets of God, Latter-day Saints fast one day each month and contribute generously to a fast offering fund at least the equivalent of the meals forfeited and often many times more. Such sacred offerings finance the operation of storehouses, supply cash needs of the poor, and provide medical care for the sick who are without funds.

In many areas, the offerings are collected each month by the boys who are deacons, as they visit each member's home, generally quite early on the Sabbath day. I recall that the boys in the congregation over which I presided had assembled one morning, sleepy-eyed, a bit disheveled, and mildly complaining about arising so early to fulfill their assignment. Not a word of reproof was spoken, but during the following week, we escorted the boys to Welfare Square for a guided tour. They saw firsthand a lame person operating the telephone switchboard, an older man stocking shelves, women arranging clothing to be distributed—even a blind person placing labels on cans. Here were individuals earning their sustenance through their contributed labors. A penetrating silence came over the boys as they witnessed how their efforts each month helped to collect the sacred fast offering funds that aided the needy and provided employment for those who otherwise would be idle.

From that hallowed day forward, there was no urging required by our deacons. On fast Sunday mornings they were present at seven o'clock, dressed in their Sunday best, anxious to do their duty as holders of the Aaronic Priesthood. No longer were they simply distributing and collecting envelopes. They were helping to provide food for the hungry and shelter for the homeless—all after the way of the Lord. Their smiles were more frequent, their pace more eager, their very souls more subdued. Perhaps now they were marching to the beat of a different drummer; perhaps now they better understood the classic passage, "Inasmuch as ye have done it unto one of the least of these my brethren, ye have done it unto me." (Matthew 25:40.)

To the third and final question, "What prompts such devotion on the part of every worker?" the answer can be stated simply: an individual testimony of the gospel of the Lord Jesus Christ, even a heartfelt desire to love the Lord with all one's heart, mind, and soul, and one's neighbor as oneself.

This is what motivated a personal friend who was in the produce business to telephone me during those days as a bishop and say, "I'm sending to the storehouse a semitruck and trailer filled with citrus fruits for those who would otherwise go without. Let the storehouse management know the truck is coming, and there will be no charge; but Bishop, no one is to know who sent it." Rarely have I seen the joy and appreciation this generous act brought forth. Never have I questioned the eternal reward to which that unnamed benefactor, since deceased, has now gone.

Such kind deeds of generosity are not a rarity, but are frequently found. Situated beneath the heavily traveled freeway that girds Salt Lake City is the home of a sixty-year-old single man who has, due to a crippling disease, never known a day without pain nor many days without loneliness. One winter's day as I visited him, he was slow in answering the doorbell's ring. I entered his well-kept home; the temperature in save but one room, the kitchen, was a chilly forty degrees. The reason: insufficient money to heat any other room. The walls needed papering, the ceiling to be lowered, the cupboards to be filled.

Troubled by the experience of visiting my friend, a bishop was consulted and a miracle of love, prompted by testimony, took place. The ward members were organized and the labor of love was begun. A month later, my friend, Lou, called and asked if I would come and see what had happened to him. I did, and indeed beheld a miracle. The sidewalks, which had been uprooted by poplar trees, had been replaced, the porch of the home rebuilt, a new door with glistening hardware installed, the ceilings lowered, the walls papered, the woodwork painted, the roof replaced, and the cupboards filled. No longer was the home chilly and uninviting. It now seemed to whisper a warm welcome. Lou saved until last showing me his pride and joy: there on his bed was a beautiful plaid quilt bearing the crest of his Scottish family clan. It had been made with loving care by the women of the Relief Society. Before leaving, I discovered that each week the Young Adults were to bring in a hot dinner and share a home evening. Warmth had replaced the cold; repairs had transformed the wear of years; but more significantly, hope had dispelled despair and now love reigned triumphant.

All who participated in this moving drama of real life had discovered a new and personal appreciation of the Master's teaching, "It is more blessed to give than to receive." (Acts 20:35.)

The welfare plan of The Church of Jesus Christ of Latter-day Saints is inspired of Almighty God. Indeed, the Lord Jesus Christ is its architect. To all there is extended a sincere invitation: Come to Salt Lake City and visit Welfare Square. Your eyes will glow a little brighter, your heart will beat a little faster, and life itself will acquire a new depth of meaning.

27

The Spirit of Christmas

Christmas, however old, is forever new. The Christmas season can be truly meaningful if we but let it be. One Christmas my little son stood before the fireplace and recited what he thought was a new poem. He said, "Daddy, I've learned a new poem and I'd like to teach it to you. I know you'll like it." The poem he then recited commenced: " 'Twas the night before Christmas, when all through the house,/Not a creature was stirring, not even a mouse." (Clement C. Moore, "A Visit from St. Nicholas.") And on he went. He said, "Isn't that a wonderful poem, Daddy?" I had an opportunity to tell him it *was* a wonderful poem, because almost everything I associate with Christmas is important to me.

On one occasion I had the privilege of taking my family downtown as Santa Claus made his appearance. It was interesting; crowds gathered. One little girl I particularly noticed had been standing on the curb for what seemed like many minutes, waiting for this great event. Just as Santa Claus was to make his entry, great throngs of people crowded in front of her, and she began to cry.

A six-foot-three man who stood by her asked, "What's the matter, dear?" She said, "I've been waiting to see Santa, and now I can't see him." The man picked her up and placed her on his shoulders, providing her a commanding view. As Santa

Claus came by, she waved her little hand toward him, and he smiled and waved back to her and to everyone else in the crowd. The little girl grabbed the hair of that great big fellow and exclaimed, "He saw me! He saw me and smiled at me! I'm so glad it's Christmas!" That little girl had the Christmas spirit.

I thought back on another little child who, under different circumstances, had the Christmas spirit. As a very young elder I went with a companion to the old Primary Children's Hospital on North Temple Street to provide blessings for the sick children. As we entered the door, we noted the Christmas tree with its bright and friendly lights. We saw carefully wrapped packages beneath its outstretched limbs. Then we went through the corridors where tiny boys and girls—some with a bandage upon an arm, some with a cast upon a leg, others with ailments that perhaps could not be cured so readily—each had a smile upon his face.

I walked toward the bedside of one little boy, and he said, "What is your name?" I told him. He said, "Will you give me a blessing?" The blessing was provided; and as we turned to leave his bedside, he said, "Thank you."

We walked a few steps and then I heard his little call: "Brother Monson." I turned. He said, "Merry Christmas to you." And a great smile flashed across his countenance. That boy had the Christmas spirit as did the little girl in downtown Salt Lake City.

This spirit of Christmas is something I would hope each of us would have within his heart and within his life, not only at this particular season but throughout the year.

I once had the privilege of going to Atlanta, Georgia, and seeing the church where Peter Marshall presided. I thought of his declaration and his urging when he spoke to the people and pleaded: "Let us not *spend* Christmas and let us not *observe* Christmas, necessarily, but let us *keep* Christmas in our hearts and in our lives." This would be my plea today, for when we keep the spirit of Christmas we keep the spirit of Christ, because the Christmas spirit is the Christ spirit.

One who had keen insight into the Christmas spirit wrote:

"I am the Christmas Spirit. I enter the home of poverty and cause pale-faced children to open wide their eyes in pleased wonder. I cause the miser to release his clutched hand, thus painting a bright spot upon his soul.

"I cause the aged to remember their youth and to laugh in the glad old way. I bring romance to childhood and brighten dreams woven with magic.

"I cause eager feet to climb dark stairways with filled baskets, leaving behind hearts amazed at the goodness of the world.

"I cause the prodigal to pause in his wild and wasteful way and send to anxious love some little token which releases glad tears, washing away the hard lines of sorrow.

"I enter dark prison cells, causing scarred manhood to remember what might have been and pointing to better days yet to come.

"I enter the still, white home of pain, and there lips that are too weak to speak just tremble in silent, eloquent gratitude.

"In a thousand ways I cause this weary old world to look up into the face of God and for a few minutes forget everything that is small and wretched. You see, I am the Christmas Spirit." (Author Unknown.)

This is the spirit I pray we might have, because when we have the spirit of Christmas we remember Him whose birth we commemorate at this season of the year. We remember that first Christmas day—a day that was prophesied by the prophets of old. You, with me, recall the words of Isaiah, when he said, "Behold, a virgin shall conceive, and bear a son,

185

and shall call his name Immanuel." (Isaiah 7:14.) Again Isaiah declared: "For unto us a child is born, . . . and his name shall be called . . . The Prince of Peace." (Isaiah 9:6.)

On the American continent, the prophets said: "The time cometh, and is not far distant, that with power, the Lord Omnipotent . . . shall dwell in a tabernacle of clay. . . . And lo, he shall suffer temptations, and pain. . . . And he shall be called Jesus Christ, the Son of God." (Mosiah 3:5, 7-8.)

Then came that night of nights when the shepherds were abiding in the fields and the angel of the Lord appeared to them, announcing, "Fear not: for, behold, I bring you good tidings of great joy. . . . For unto you is born this day in the city of David a Saviour, which is Christ the Lord." (Luke 2:10-11.) The shepherds went with haste to the manger to pay honor to Christ the Lord. Wise men journeyed from the East to Jerusalem, saying: "Where is he that is born King of the Jews? for we have seen his star in the east, and are come to worship him. . . . When they saw the star, they rejoiced with exceeding great joy. And when they were come into the house, they saw the young child with Mary his mother, and fell down, and worshipped him: and when they had opened their treasures, they presented unto him gifts; gold, and frankincense, and myrrh." (Matthew 2:2, 10-11.)

Since that time, the spirit of giving gifts has been present in the mind of each Christian as he commemorates the Christmas season. I wonder if we might profit today by asking ourselves, "What gift would God have me give to Him or to others at this precious season of the year?"

I feel that I might answer that question and declare in all solemnity that our Heavenly Father would want each one of His children to render unto Him a gift of obedience so that we would actually love the Lord our God with all our hearts, all our minds, and all our strength. Then, I am sure, He would expect us to love our neighbors as ourselves.

I would not be surprised were He to instruct us to give of ourselves and not be selfish, nor greedy, nor contentious, nor quarrelsome, repeating his own words in Third Nephi, when He said, "And there shall be no disputations among you. . . . For verily, verily I say unto you, . . . contention is not of me, but is of the devil, who . . . stirreth up the hearts of men to contend with anger, one with another. Behold, this is not my doctrine, to stir up the hearts of men with anger, . . . but this is my doctrine, that such things should be done away." (3 Nephi 11:28-30.)

So I would plead with all to rid from our lives any spirit of contention, any spirit wherein we might vie one with another for the spoils of life, but rather that we might cooperatively work with our brethren and with our sisters for the fruits of the gospel of Jesus Christ.

I trust that we will not forget at this Christmas season the gratitude that must be within our hearts and that yearns to be expressed. I hope that no one will take his birthright for granted. I hope that youth, particularly, will not forget mother or father, but rather that we might honor our fathers and honor our mothers. What finer Christmas gift could they receive than to know that a son or a daughter was honoring them by honoring God and living the commandments of the gospel of Jesus Christ?

Recently I was in Corpus Christi, Texas. A proud father came forward to me and slipped into my hand a letter from his son serving a mission in Australia. I would like to share this letter with you. It may provide the format whereby you might write a similar letter to your parents as an extra Christmas gift this year. The letter reads:

Dear Mom and Dad,

I want to thank you from the bottom of my heart for the many wonderful things you have done for me. I want to thank you for listening to the message the elders presented to you when they knocked at your door, and thank you for the way you grasped the gospel and made it the mold around which you shaped your lives and the lives of your children. I love each of you very much.

Thank you for the way you taught me, for the love which you expressed in many ways. Thank you for directing me in the right pathways, for showing me instead of forcing me. I am thankful for your beautiful testimonies and for the guiding love in which you helped me gain mine. I know the gospel is true. My few experiences here have strengthened my testimony. I pray that I might live up to your expectations, and with God's help, I will.

Thank you again, Mom and Dad.

Your loving son,
David

What finer expression could a boy give his parents than the gift of gratitude? I would hope that, in addition to the gift of gratitude that we bestow upon our parents, we remember that our loved ones—our brothers, our sisters, our relatives, our friends, those with whom we mingle and associate—can benefit and be profited if we give of ourselves in helping them to see the truth and helping them around the quicksands of life that would claim them if only those quicksands could. I would hope that we might be able to light a spark in the lives of others and enable them to see their possibilities, rather than the problems that beset them day by day.

I would hope that we would become expert in the field of human relations. Mr. Robert Woodruff, a great American industrialist, went from one end of this country to the other telling us how we might better get along with one another. He developed what he called a "Capsule Course in Human Relations." He taught:

"The five most important words in the English language are these: *I am proud of you.*

"The four most important words in the English language are these: *What is your opinion?*

"The three most important words are: *If you please.*

"The two most important words are: *Thank you.*

"The least important word of all is: *I.*"

Isn't that the spirit of Christmas, really—to forget self and to think of others? I clipped an item taken from the diary of Mrs. Rebecca Riter, entered December 26, 1847. She describes that first Christmas in the Valley of the Great Salt Lake: "The winter was cold. Christmas came, and the children were hungry. I had brought a peck of wheat across the plains and had hidden it under a pile of wood. I thought I would cook a handful of wheat for the baby. Then I thought how we would need wheat for seed in the spring, so I left it alone."

In our bounteous lives, we may well reflect upon the more meager Christmas seasons of our pioneer ancestors. We might say to ourselves, "But that was yesterday. What about today? Have times changed? Is everyone so well off that he doesn't need the real spirit of Christmas?"

To this I would answer, Times have *not* changed. The commandments of God are the same. The principles of gratitude and of giving of oneself are the same, because today, like yesterday, there are hearts to gladden and there are lives to cheer and there are blessings to bestow upon our fellow-men.

Some might say, "I am ill-equipped; my talents are so few." Then I would ask them to take a short journey with me—a journey to a hospital in Salt Lake City, the University Hospital, where I had the privilege of being summoned to the side of a man who was in danger of dying. As I walked to the hospital ward, I noted the sign on the doorway: "Intensive Care—Enter only upon permission of the head nurse." I sought the required permission and then went to the bedside of this good man.

The great machines of medical science were by his side, mechanically taking over when his heart would falter. An oxy-

189

gen mask covered his face. He turned his face toward me, but there was no glimmer of recognition in his eyes, because the man in whose presence I stood was totally blind. Yet, as he heard my voice and thought back on more pleasant times, tears began to stream from those sightless eyes and he asked a blessing from one who held the priesthood of God.

At the conclusion of that blessing I recalled how this man had been blessed with a beautiful voice. While he was not a regular attender at church, he would come—particularly on Mother's Day—and sing that beautiful number, "Mother McCree," and other songs honoring mothers. No one who ever heard him sing left without a greater appreciation for his own mother, resulting in his honoring her and all womanhood. Similarly he would participate in Christmas programs and would sing "O Holy Night." No person who heard him sing this song came away without dedicating his life to better serving the Lord and *keeping* Christmas, rather than *spending* Christmas.

The thought came into my heart that here was a man who, in his own humble way, had used the talent God had given him to bring joy and happiness into the lives of others. Multiply his talent (a beautiful voice) with the talents we possess—eyes that see, ears that hear, and hearts that know and feel—and then think where our Christmas opportunity might be this very year. It may come at a time when we least expect it.

This is the spirit of Christmas, the spirit I ask that we carry in our hearts. Let us remember the words of Charles Dickens recalling old Marley's ghost appearing to Ebenezer Scrooge: "Not to know that any Christian spirit working in its little sphere, whatever it may be, will find its mortal life too short for its vast means of usefulness. Not to know that no space of regret can make amends for one life's opportunities misused! Yet such was I! Oh! Such was I!"

And then Marley added: "At this time of the rolling year I suffer most. Why did I walk through crowds of fellow beings with my eyes turned down, and never raise them to that blessed Star which guided the Wise Men to a poor abode! Were there no poor homes to which its light might have conducted *me!*" ("A Christmas Carol.")

May we learn a lesson from the pen of Dickens and from the words of Jesus Christ. May we lift our eyes heavenward and look upward and outward into the lives of others. May we remember each Christmas season that it is more blessed to give than to receive.

In so doing, the spirit of Christ, which is the spirit of Christmas, will find a place in our hearts and in our lives, and we will feel to say, "This has been the finest Christmas ever."

28

*K*now How—Tell How—Show How

When Jesus walked and taught among men during the meridian of time, the Sadducees and the Pharisees tried constantly to twist the meaning of His words and the purpose of His teachings. Such was the desire of the inquiring lawyer, who stepped from the crowd and asked Him a question, tempting Him, and saying, "Master, which is the great commandment in the law?" Jesus said unto him, "Thou shalt love the Lord thy God with all thy heart, and with all thy soul, and with all thy mind. This is the first and great commandment. And the second is like unto it. Thou shalt love thy neighbour as thyself. On these two commandments hang all the law and the prophets." (Matthew 22:36-40.)

If you or I were there, we might then have asked, "Master, how might we best show our love?" Perhaps we would have heard the words, "He that hath my commandments, and keepeth them, he it is that loveth me." (John 14:21.) Or, "If ye love me, keep my commandments." (John 14:15.)

Another question: "How might I best show my love for my fellowmen?" And the words of King Benjamin could well apply: "When ye are in the service of your fellow beings ye are only in the service of your God." (Mosiah 2:17.) Service is the best measuring stick of love.

Each of us has many opportunities to serve. We have the

privilege of demonstrating how well we love the Lord, our God, and our fellowmen. I fear that at times we look upon our calls to serve as routine, matter of fact, and maybe some even question the inspiration that prompted a particular call. I know that stake presidents and bishops who make such calls live close to God and earnestly pray for direction, realizing that the youth of the Church are certain to be affected thereby.

Well do I remember the inspiration that attended the call to a ward president of Young Men. As a bishopric, my counselors and I knelt and prayed for inspiration in the selection of a new president. We reviewed the names of the priesthood holders, but no name seemed to be the right one. The matter was deferred. The next day I was riding a bus south on Main Street in Salt Lake City; my mind was upon our youth problems. I felt prompted to turn and look out one of the windows of that bus, and there saw a former member of our ward walking in front of the old Post Office Building. His name was Jack, and I thought, "If only Jack still lived in our ward, what an excellent president he would make!" In our next bishopric meeting, I mentioned this experience to my counselors, and one of them replied, "Bishop, did you know that Jack has moved back into the ward?" We went immediately to his home and explained the circumstances pertinent to his call. Of course he accepted and served most capably. As a result of his service there was a special blessing bestowed. He met and fell in love with a counselor in the stake Young Women, and a temple marriage resulted. Should you today ask Jack or Evelyn the greatest decision in their lives, they would reply, "The day Jack accepted an inspired call to serve the Lord."

Such is the inspiration that attends our calls to serve. When this fact is understood, we then desire with all our hearts to serve well, that joy may attend our efforts and success crown our labors.

To help us achieve this goal, I have chosen to describe

three experts who can assist me. They are men of sound judgment, men of experience, men who have proved themselves successful in youth leadership. May I present the How brothers: Know How, Tell How, and Show How. These brothers are somewhat like Siamese triplets, in that they are inseparable from one another, but more importantly, they are indispensable to us.

First, may I introduce Know How, since he will help us to obtain a proper foundation and background for our assignments. The expression "Knowledge is power" is attributed to Francis Bacon, but it had its origin long before his time, in the saying of Solomon that "a wise man is strong; yea, a man of knowledge increaseth strength." (Proverbs 24:5.)

Do we have a knowledge of our particular assignments? Do we know what is expected of us? Do we really know those who serve under our direction, that we might provide guidance and counsel for them? But above and beyond this knowledge, do we know the gospel? "And this is life eternal, that they might know thee the only true God, and Jesus Christ, whom thou hast sent." (John 17:3.)

Such knowledge will dispel that hidden and insidious enemy who lurks within and limits our capacity, destroys our initiative, and strangles our effectiveness. This enemy of whom I speak is fear: a fear to wholeheartedly accept a calling; a fear to provide direction to others; a fear to lead, to motivate, to inspire. In His wisdom, the Lord provided a formula whereby we might overcome the archvillain of fear. He instructed: "If ye are prepared ye shall not fear." (D&C 38:30.)

May I now formally introduce to you another of the How brothers, Tell How. He always follows his brother Know How. This way his message finds greater acceptance. To have knowledge and to know and understand an objective is one thing, but it is another matter altogether to inspire others with this same knowledge and understanding. To properly communicate to others our ideas, our hopes, and our goals requires skill and teamwork. No one serves the Lord alone. No assignment is an island by itself. The Lord's organization provides the Lord's help.

Our instructions are best understood and followed when we ourselves know where we are going. In an Eastern school where leadership was confused and stumbling, a thoughtful youth lamented: "We're asked to follow our leaders, but they don't know where they are going, or how to get there." When we know our goals and enthusiastically tell our co-workers where we are expected to go, what we are expected to do, and when and how we are expected to do it, the response is spontaneous. The apostle Peter emphasized effective communications when he urged, "Sanctify the Lord God in your hearts: and be ready always to give an answer to every man that asketh you a reason of the hope that is in you." (1 Peter 3:15.)

A number of years ago when a very prominent national figure was defeated for a high public office, he said, "I did not communicate effectively." This has been the experience of large numbers of unsuccessful parents, teachers, and youth. Programs can be frustrated, organizations weakened, even eternal lives lost when leaders in the Church do not get their messages over to those for whom they have responsibility. Just as we need Know How, we cannot do without Tell How.

May I now present our final How brother, Show How. He demonstrates his effectiveness wherever he happens to be. "Come follow me" continues as the most persuasive leadership phrase ever given. When the Lord gave this invitation to Peter, to Phillip, and to the Levite at receipt of customs, each followed. They knew and were yet to learn even more convincingly that Jesus, their leader, asked no sacrifice, demanded no service, required no effort beyond that which He Himself so willingly gave. He cautioned all of us in leadership positions that we are presiding servants and not presiding masters. Remember, when we as leaders serve, others will serve. When we tithe, others tithe. When we comply with God's laws, others do likewise.

Will you take the How brothers with you in your assignment? Know How will dispel fear. Tell How will instill confidence. Show How will inspire others to follow. Their teachings were demonstrated when Gideon of old faced his most crucial test. You will recall that Gideon and his followers came upon an overwhelmingly superior force of Midianites and Amalekites. The enemy lay in the valley like grasshoppers for multitude, and their camels without number as the sand by the seaside for multitude. Gideon needed knowledge to extricate himself from this frightful situation.

To his amazement, the Lord said unto him: "The people that are with thee are too many for me to give the Midianites into their hands, lest Israel vaunt themselves against me, saying, Mine own hand hath saved me. Now therefore go to, proclaim in the ears of the people, saying, Whosoever is fearful and afraid, let him return and depart early from mount Gilead. And there returned of the people twenty and two thousand; and there remained ten thousand."

Again the Lord ruled that Gideon had too many followers, and instructed him to take them to water to observe the manner in which they should drink of the water. Those who lapped the water were placed in one group, and those who bowed down upon their knees to drink were placed in another. The Lord said unto Gideon, "By the three hundred men that lapped will I save you, and deliver the Midianites into thine hand: and let all the other people go every man unto his place."

A battle plan was provided. The force was to be divided into three companies. Trumpets were to be taken in the right hand and a pitcher containing a lamp within the other hand. The Know How had been provided. Now Gideon supplied the

Tell How. He said, "When I blow with a trumpet, I and all that are with me, then blow ye the trumpets also on every side of all the camp, and say, The sword of the Lord, and of Gideon." He then said in effect, "Follow me." His exact words were, "As I do, so shall ye do." Show How was now an integral part of his leadership. At the leader's signal, the host of Gideon did blow on the trumpets and did break the pitchers and did shout, "The sword of the Lord, and of Gideon." The scripture records the outcome of this decisive battle: "And they stood every man in his place," and the battle was won. (Judges 7:2-21.)

As we stand and serve in our appointed places, eternal victory may be ours and theirs whom we have been privileged to lead.

Index

A

Aaron, Hank, 172-73
Adam, 38, 82, 126
Affluence, poverty of, 92-93
Airplane landing in storm, 27
Alcott, Louisa May, 169
America: God's promises
concerning, 95; needs righteous
people, 99
"America the Beautiful," 95
Apostasy, 10
Army of righteousness,
priesthood is, 58
Art galleries, 1
Athlete, paralysis of, 161
Australia, 143

B

Ballard, Melvin J., 24
Baseball, 37, 172-73
Battle fought by Gideon, 197-98
"Be Attitudes," 122
Beatitudes, Mount of, 9

"Behold, a Royal Army," 57-58
Bell of church, boy recognizes
peal of, 14
Belshazzar, 91
Bible, translation of, into
English, 10-11
Bishopric, choosing between
Navy and, 135-36
Bishop's storehouse, 177
Blessings depend on obedience,
102
Blessings, priesthood: given to
girl with amputated leg, 21-22;
given to girl suffering from
cancer, 34-35; given to fellow
seaman, 62; given to
hospitalized child at
Christmas, 184
Blind father rescues daughter
from drowning, 173
Boats: toy, 46; paper, 155-56
Boy Scout conference, 21
Brigham Young University,
letter to, commending
students, 66-67

Diligence, serving with, 147

Disappointment, Christ knew, 108-9

Dispensation of the Fulness of Times, 13

Dog: boy sold, for $50,000, 120; grandfather's scolding over, 162

Drowning daughter saved by blind father, 173

Drunkenness among youth, 90

Dryden, John, 121

Dutch family requests missionary lessons, 129-30

Duty, learning and fulfilling, 93, 147, 172

E

Earthquake, missionary hurt in, 49-50

Education, importance of, 84

Effort, continuous, 47

Eisenhower, Dwight D., 127

Elijah, 3-4

Ellsworth, Randall, 49-50

Emerald of king, search for, 171-72

Engh, Edward, 164-65

Enthusiasm, 118

Evil: distinguishing good from, 84; strength to combat, comes through obedience, 105

Exaltation, formula for, 168

Examples: following, 40-41; parents must set, 77, 84, 88; set by European immigrant,

103-5; leaders must set, 122

F

Faith: of child at mother's funeral, 6-7; importance of, in fulfilling Church callings, 19, 116; creates heroes, 40; in personal God, 97; making decisions concerning, 128-29; of Tahitian people, 134; finding, 159; of little children, 160; cannot coexist with doubt, 162

Family, strength of, 77-78

Fast offerings, 180

Father, letter to, urging him to stop smoking, 29

Fear, overcoming, 195

Field, Eugene, 35-36

Fig tree, parable, of, 168

Financing of Church welfare plan, 179-80

Firmness in face of sin, 19-20

First vision of Joseph Smith, 12-13

Football player, paralysis of, 161

Ford, Henry, 84, 121

Formula for exaltation, 168

Formula "W," 117

Fosdick, Harry Emerson, 59

Foundations, importance of strong, 83

Fountain of youth, search for, 17

Fox, Ruth May, 20

Q

R

Race, life likened to, 46
Reformation, day of, 10-12
Respect of youth for parents, 77
Responsibility: involved in free agency, 82; of parents toward children, 84-85, 87; leadership involves, 144
Restoration of gospel, 12-13
Resurrection: reality of, 5-6; Christ's promise concerning, 36
Rigdon, Sidney, 6
Road: to Jericho, 153-54; to glory, 165
Royal army, priesthood is, 58
Russell, Bertrand, 2
Ruth, 39

S

Sacrifice, obedience is better than, 102, 110
St. George, temple workers in, 55-56
Salt Lake City, 177
Samuel, 102
San Francisco *Examiner* editorial, 90-91
Santa Claus, 183-84
Satan: seeks to lead away God's elect, 48; tempted Christ, 103, 109; makes evil seem good, 119
Schopenhaur, 2
Schumann-Heink, Madame Ernestine, 76
Scriptures: testify of God's love,

81-82; examples in, of important decisions, 126
Serra, James, 34
Service, desires for, 59; Christ set example of, 110, 154; willingness in, 146-47; diligence in, 147; filling one's life with, 169-70; is best measuring stick of love, 193
Sharpe, R.L., 128
"Shall the Youth of Zion Falter," 65, 71
Shepherds vs. sheepherders, 144
Shreveport, Louisiana, 32-33
Show How, 196
Sin, burden of, 98
Skidmore, Mark, 69
Skilled labor, 83
Smith, George Albert, 117
Smith, Joseph, 6, 12-13, 39, 127
Souls, worth of, 81, 115
Stake conference assignments, 27-28, 33, 143
Stake missionaries, calling of, 123-24
Stake presidency, call to serve in, 57
Stamp collection, 68
Staples, Elgin, 26
Stauffer family, 79-80
Stephen, 5
Stephens, Evan, 65
Stepping-stones vs. stumbling blocks, 128
Stevenson, Robert Louis, 1

Index

Story, boy begs father to tell, 85-86
Success, paying price of, 48
Sudbury, Craig, 41-42
Sudbury, Fred, 41-42
"Suffer the little children to come unto me," 32, 34
Sunday dinner delivered to "Old Bob," 163
Sunday School: unruly class in, 149; special teacher of, 149-51; superintendent of, helped poor boy, 155-56

T

Tahitian people, 134
Talents: parable of, 167; using, to enrich others, 190
Teachers quorum president, 61
Teamwork, 122, 196
Tell How, 195-96
Temple: widows called to work in, 4; *New Era* issue about, 21-22; families sealed in, 29, 54, 79-80; at Logan, Utah, 53-54; at New Zealand, 54; pictures of, in children's bedrooms, 54; touching door of, 55; importance of attending, 55; workers in, dropped clothes in mud, 55-56
Temptations: of today's youth, 90-91; Christ overcame, 103, 109
Testimonies: borne at youth conference, 20; helping youths acquire, 93; responsibility of

gaining, 129-30
"Thanks for the Sabbath School," 151
Thinking: taking time for, 19; is man's hardest work, 84; big, 120-21
Time, preciousness of, 82, 169
Toy boats, 46
Train, electric, 157-58
Travel brochure, 107
Treasures left by mother, 78
"True Nobility," poem, 147
Truth: brings comfort, 5-6; restoration of, to earth, 12-13; stand firm for, 19-20; power of, 77-78; definition of, 101; filling one's mind with, 168-69
" 'Twas the Night Before Christmas," 183
Twohig, Daniel S., 108
Tyndale, William, 11-12

U

Ullman, Samuel, 18
Understanding, leaders must be, 148
Unselfishness, gift of, 187

V

Values, distortion of, 146
Virgins, ten, parable of, 167
Vocation, choosing, 132-33

W

"W" formula, 117

208

Walking in Christ's footsteps, 108

Washington, George, statue of, 24

Water, names associated with, 143

Wealth is not satisfying, 91-92

Welfare plan of Church: operation of, 178-79; financing of, 179-80; devotion of workers in, 181-82

Welfare Square, 177

"What Is Home," poem, 76

Widow: of Zarephath, 3-4; of Nain, 4; in Salt Lake City, 4; two mites of, 68; Navajo, 111; helping, through Church welfare plan, 178

Wife, future, meeting with, 131

Willingness to serve, importance of, 146-47

Wolsey, Cardinal, 146-47

Woodruff, Robert, 188-89

Work: value of, 116-17; leadership requires, 122

World: accent of, on youth, 17; rapid changes in, 75, 120; decline in morals of, 76, 90-91, 145; picture of, torn and reassembled, 85-86; competitive nature of, 126

World War II, 26, 62-63;

enlistment poster of, 99; momentous decisions of, 127-28, 132

Worth of souls, 81, 115

Wycliffe, John, 10-11

Y

Yankee Stadium, 37

"You," poem, 48

Young Men's president, calling of, 194

Young Women's president asks to be released, 19

Youth: worldly accent on, 17; retaining spirit of, 18; wickedness among, 18, 90; guidelines for leaders of, 19-22; 145; problems facing, 65-66; loneliness among, 81; is time of preparation, 82-83; hope of, 89; helping, to acquire testimonies, 93; beauty of, 125; are faced with monumental decisions, 126, 128; should not choose easiest way, 133

Youth conference, 20

Z

Zarephath, widow at, 3-4

Zwingli, 11